Understanding GenAI: From Basics to Ethical Implications

Fernando Abednego Halim

First Edition

2024

Disclaimer

This book contains AI-generated content. While every effort has been made to ensure the accuracy and completeness of the information, the nature of AI-generated content means that there may be inaccuracies or omissions. Readers are advised to validate the truthfulness and reliability of the content before applying or using it. The authors and publisher disclaim any liability in connection with the use of this information.

First Edition: 2024

ISBN-13: 979-8-3321-7811-5

To all the innovators, dreamers, and pioneers in the field of artificial intelligence who continuously push the boundaries of what is possible.

To our readers, who seek knowledge and understanding, and to the future generations who will build upon these foundations to create a better world.

And finally, to my families and friends, for their unwavering support and encouragement throughout this journey.

Contents

Introduction

Embracing the Future of Generative AI

Welcome to *Understanding GenAI: From Basics to Ethical Implications*, a comprehensive guide to the fascinating world of Generative AI. This book is your gateway to exploring the transformative potential of artificial intelligence, a field that is reshaping industries, enhancing human creativity, and pushing the boundaries of what is possible.

Why Generative AI?

Generative AI represents one of the most exciting advancements in technology today. Unlike traditional AI systems that analyze and predict, Generative AI creates. It generates new content—whether it's text, images, music, or even entire virtual worlds—by learning from existing data. This ability to create and innovate opens up a multitude of possibilities across various domains.

From creating stunning works of art and composing music to revolutionizing healthcare and driving innovation in gaming, Generative AI is making its mark in ways that were once the realm of science fiction. But with great power comes great responsibility. As we delve into the capabilities of Generative AI, it is crucial to understand the ethical considerations that come with it.

What to Expect from This Book

This book is designed to take you on a journey through the world of Generative AI, starting with its foundational concepts and leading you through its applications, ethical implications, and future trends. Whether you are a seasoned AI professional, a student eager to learn, or simply someone curious about the future of technology, this book offers valuable insights and practical knowledge.

- **Chapter 1: The Dawn of Generative AI** traces the historical context and evolution of AI, setting the stage for the emergence of generative models.

- **Chapter 2: Fundamentals of Machine Learning** provides a deep dive into the essential concepts of machine learning, the backbone of Generative AI.

- **Chapter 3: Understanding Neural Networks and Deep Learning** explores the architectures and mechanisms that power modern AI systems.

- **Chapter 4: Generative Models and Their Types** introduces you to various generative models, including GANs, VAEs, and more, explaining how they work and their applications.

- **Chapter 5: Applications of Generative AI** showcases the real-world impact of Generative AI across different industries.

- **Chapter 6: Ethical Implications of Generative AI** addresses the critical ethical concerns and responsibilities that come with the power of AI.

- **Chapter 7: Mitigating Bias and Ensuring Fairness** discusses strategies to reduce bias and promote fairness in AI systems.

- **Chapter 8: Future Trends in Generative AI** looks ahead to the emerging trends and innovations that will shape the future of AI.

- **Chapter 9: Building Your Own Generative AI Models** provides practical guidance on creating and training your own generative models.

- **Chapter 10: The Ethical AI Movement and Your Role** emphasizes the importance of ethical AI practices and how you can contribute to this vital movement.

Why This Book Matters

As we venture further into the age of AI, understanding and responsibly harnessing its capabilities is more important than ever. This book aims to equip you with the knowledge to appreciate the potential of Generative AI while being mindful of its ethical implications. By fostering a deeper understanding, we can collectively ensure that AI serves to enhance human life, foster creativity, and build a fairer, more inclusive world.

A Journey of Discovery

Embarking on this journey, you will discover not only the technical intricacies of Generative AI but also the profound ways it intersects with our lives and society. You will learn how to build and utilize these powerful models and explore the broader implications of their use. Most importantly, you will gain insights into how you can play a role in shaping the future of AI, ensuring that it is developed and deployed responsibly.

Join Me

Join me as we explore the fascinating world of Generative AI. Together, we will delve into its foundations, celebrate its achievements, navigate its challenges, and envision a future where AI empowers us to reach new heights. Your journey into the world of Generative AI begins here.

Welcome to *Understanding GenAI: From Basics to Ethical Implications*. Let's embark on this exciting adventure together.

Chapter 1

The Dawn of Generative AI

A Technological Renaissance

The emergence of Generative AI signifies a monumental leap in technology, heralding a new era where machines can create, innovate, and generate content with human-like proficiency. From its humble beginnings, artificial intelligence (AI) has grown exponentially, achieving feats that once seemed the stuff of science fiction. This chapter delves into the historical context, tracing the evolution of AI from simple rule-based systems to complex generative models, and explores the revolutionary impact of these advancements on various aspects of our lives.

The Genesis of Artificial Intelligence

The concept of artificial intelligence dates back to ancient myths and stories where inventors dreamt of creating artificial beings imbued with human-like intelligence. However, the modern field of AI began to take shape in the mid-20th century. In 1956, the term "artificial intelligence" was coined at the Dartmouth Conference, marking the birth of AI as an academic discipline. Early AI research focused on developing systems that could perform logical reasoning and problem-solving tasks. These systems, known as rule-based systems or expert systems, relied on predefined rules and logic to make decisions (McCarthy et al. 2006).

Rule-Based Systems: The Early Days

Rule-based systems represented the first wave of AI technology. These systems used a set of "if-then" rules to mimic human decision-making processes. While they were effective in narrow domains such as medical diagnosis and financial analysis, their reliance on explicitly programmed rules limited their flexibility and adaptability. Despite these limitations, rule-based systems laid the foundation for future AI research by demonstrating that machines could replicate certain aspects of human intelligence (Feigenbaum and Barr 1983).

The Advent of Machine Learning

The next significant milestone in the evolution of AI was the advent of machine learning (ML). Unlike rule-based systems, machine learning algorithms could learn from data and improve their performance over time. This paradigm shift was made possible by the increasing availability of digital data and advances in computational power. In the 1980s and 1990s, researchers developed various ML techniques, including decision trees, support vector machines, and neural networks (Quinlan 1986; Cortes and Vapnik 1995; LeCun, Boser, et al. 1989). These algorithms enabled machines to recognize patterns, classify data, and make predictions with remarkable accuracy. Machine learning fundamentally changed the landscape of AI by allowing systems to be trained on data rather than being explicitly programmed. This approach led to more adaptable and robust AI systems capable of handling a wider range of tasks and scenarios.

Neural Networks: The Building Blocks of AI

Neural networks, inspired by the structure and function of the human brain, became a cornerstone of modern AI. Early neural networks, such as perceptrons, could perform simple tasks like binary classification. However, their capabilities were limited by computational constraints and the lack of efficient training algorithms. The development of backpropagation in the 1980s, a method for training multi-layer neural networks, marked a breakthrough in neural network research (Rumelhart, Geoffrey E. Hinton, and Ronald J. Williams 1986). This advancement allowed neural networks to learn more complex patterns and perform tasks such as image recognition and speech processing. The architecture of neural networks, consisting of interconnected layers of artificial neurons, enabled the modeling of complex non-linear relationships in data. This capability was crucial for advancing AI beyond simple rule-based systems.

The Rise of Deep Learning

The 21st century witnessed the rise of deep learning, a subfield of machine learning that focuses on training deep neural networks with many layers. Deep learning models, such as convolutional neural networks (CNNs) and recurrent neural networks (RNNs), achieved unprecedented success in various domains, including computer vision, natural language processing, and game playing. The availability of large datasets and powerful GPUs enabled researchers to train deep learning models with billions of parameters, leading to state-of-the-art performance on numerous tasks (Krizhevsky, Sutskever, and Geoffrey E. Hinton 2012; Sutskever, Vinyals, and Quoc V. Le 2014). Deep learning marked a significant shift in AI capabilities, allowing machines to learn from vast amounts of unstructured data and perform tasks with human-like accuracy. This advancement set the stage for the development of generative models capable of creating new content.

Generative AI: A New Frontier

Generative AI represents a new frontier in the evolution of artificial intelligence. Unlike traditional AI systems that focus on classification and prediction, generative models aim to create new data that is indistinguishable from real data. This capability opens up a wide range of possibilities, from generating realistic images and videos to composing music and writing poetry. The development of generative models such as Generative Adversarial Networks (GANs) and Variational Autoencoders (VAEs) has revolutionized the field of AI by demonstrating that machines can exhibit creativity and innovation.

Generative Adversarial Networks (GANs)

Introduced by Ian (I. Goodfellow, Pouget-Abadie, et al. 2014), GANs have become one of the most influential architectures in generative AI. GANs consist of two neural networks, a generator and a discriminator, that are trained simultaneously in a competitive setting. The generator creates fake data, while the discriminator tries to distinguish between real and fake data. Through this adversarial process, the generator learns to produce increasingly realistic data, resulting in high-quality synthetic images, videos, and other forms of content. The success of GANs lies in their ability to generate data that is virtually indistinguishable from real data. This capability has numerous applications, from creating realistic avatars for virtual environments to generating synthetic training data for machine learning models.

Variational Autoencoders (VAEs)

Variational Autoencoders (VAEs) represent another significant advancement in generative AI. VAEs are probabilistic models that learn to encode data into a latent space and then decode it back into the original space. This encoding-decoding process allows VAEs to generate new data by sampling from the latent space (Kingma and Welling 2013). VAEs have been successfully applied to various tasks, including image generation, data compression, and anomaly detection. Their ability to learn meaningful representations of data makes them powerful tools for unsupervised learning and generative modeling. VAEs offer a unique approach to generative modeling by leveraging probabilistic methods to learn and sample from the latent space. This approach enables the generation of diverse and high-quality synthetic data.

The Impact of Generative AI

The impact of Generative AI extends across numerous fields, transforming industries and enhancing human creativity. In the realm of art and entertainment, generative models are used to create original artwork, design virtual characters, and compose music. In healthcare, Generative AI aids in drug discovery, medical imaging, and personalized treatment plans. The potential applications of Generative AI are vast, offering solutions to complex problems and enabling new forms of expression and innovation.

Ethical Considerations

With the rise of Generative AI, ethical considerations have come to the forefront. The ability of generative models to create realistic content raises concerns about misinformation, privacy, and intellectual property. Deepfakes, for example, are synthetic media generated by GANs that can convincingly mimic real people, posing risks to security and trust (Chesney and Citron 2019). As Generative AI continues to evolve, it is crucial to establish ethical guidelines and frameworks to ensure its responsible use. Researchers, policymakers, and industry leaders must work together to address these challenges and harness the potential of Generative AI for the greater good.

Generative AI in Art and Creativity

Generative AI has made significant strides in the field of art, offering new tools and methods for artists to explore their creativity. Artists are now collaborating with AI to create unique pieces that blend human creativity with machine-generated patterns. Generative models can analyze existing artworks and produce new pieces that reflect similar styles, opening up new possibilities for artistic expression (Elgammal et al. 2017). AI-generated art has been exhibited in galleries and sold at auctions, challenging traditional notions of authorship and creativity. Artists like Mario Klingemann and Robbie Barrat have gained recognition for their work with generative models, demonstrating the potential of AI as a creative partner.

Generative AI in Music and Composition

In the realm of music, Generative AI is being used to compose original pieces, assist musicians in the creative process, and generate soundtracks for various applications. AI models can analyze vast collections of music and learn to generate compositions in various styles and genres. This technology enables musicians to experiment with new sounds and structures, pushing the boundaries of traditional music composition (Briot, Hadjeres, and Pachet 2020). Companies like OpenAI have developed models like MuseNet, which can compose music in the style of famous composers, blending elements from different musical traditions. These advancements are transforming the music industry, offering new tools for creativity and innovation.

Generative AI in Healthcare

Generative AI is also making significant contributions to the healthcare industry. In drug discovery, generative models can predict the properties of new compounds and suggest potential drug candidates (Zhavoronkov et al. 2019). This capability accelerates the research and development process, reducing the time and cost associated with bringing new drugs to market. In medical imaging, Generative AI can enhance the quality of scans and assist in diagnosing diseases. Models can generate high-resolution images from low-quality inputs, improving the accuracy of diagnostic tools (Baum and Agus 2020). Additionally, Generative AI is being used to create personalized treatment plans by analyzing patient data (Kaul et al. 2020) and predicting the outcomes of different interventions.

Generative AI in Gaming and Virtual Environments

The gaming industry has embraced Generative AI to create immersive and dynamic virtual environments. AI models can generate realistic landscapes, characters, and storylines, providing players with unique and engaging experiences. Procedural content generation, powered by generative models, allows game developers to create vast and varied game worlds without manually designing every element (Yannakakis and Togelius 2018). Generative AI is also being used to develop intelligent non-player characters (NPCs) that can interact with players in meaningful ways. These advancements enhance the realism and depth of virtual environments, offering players richer and more interactive experiences.

The Future of Generative AI

The future of Generative AI is filled with exciting possibilities. As models become more advanced and capable, they will continue to push the boundaries of what is possible in various fields. Researchers are exploring new architectures and training methods to improve the quality and diversity of generated content. One area of active research is the development of more interpretable and controllable generative models (P. Liu, Gao, and G. Huang 2019). These models will allow users to specify certain attributes and guide the generation process, making it easier to produce desired outcomes. Additionally, advancements in reinforcement learning and unsupervised learning are expected to further enhance the capabilities of Generative AI.

Chapter 2

Fundamentals of Machine Learning

The Heart of Artificial Intelligence

Machine learning is at the core of modern artificial intelligence, driving the advancements that enable systems to learn from data, identify patterns, and make decisions with minimal human intervention. As we delve into the world of Generative AI, understanding the fundamental concepts of machine learning is crucial. This chapter provides a comprehensive overview of machine learning, covering its basic principles, key algorithms, and essential techniques that form the foundation for more complex generative models (Mitchell 1997).

The Basics of Machine Learning

Machine learning is a subset of artificial intelligence that focuses on the development of algorithms and statistical models that enable computers to learn from and make predictions or decisions based on data. Unlike traditional programming, where a developer writes explicit instructions for the computer to follow, machine learning involves training a model on a dataset to learn the underlying patterns and relationships (Mohri, Rostamizadeh, and Talwalkar 2018).

Types of Machine Learning

Machine learning can be broadly categorized into three types: supervised learning, unsupervised learning, and reinforcement learning. Each type serves different purposes and is used to solve various types of problems (I. Goodfellow, Y. Bengio, and Courville 2016).

Supervised Learning

In supervised learning, the model is trained on a labeled dataset, meaning that each training example is paired with an output label. The goal is to learn a mapping from inputs to outputs that can be used to predict the labels of new, unseen data. Supervised learning is commonly used for tasks such as classification and regression (Friedman, Hastie, and Tibshirani 2001).

Classification

The task of classifying data into predefined categories. Examples include spam detection, image recognition, and sentiment analysis (Bishop 2006).

Regression

The task of predicting a continuous value. Examples include predicting house prices, stock prices, and temperature (Montgomery, Peck, and Vining 2012).

Unsupervised Learning

Unsupervised learning involves training a model on a dataset without labeled outputs. The goal is to find hidden patterns or structures within the data. Unsupervised learning is commonly used for tasks such as clustering, association, and dimensionality reduction (Hastie, Tibshirani, and Friedman 2009b).

Clustering

The task of grouping data points into clusters based on their similarities. Examples include customer segmentation and image segmentation (A. K. Jain, Murty, and Flynn 1999).

Association

The task of finding rules that describe large portions of the data. Examples include market basket analysis and recommendation systems (Agrawal, Imielinski, and Swami 1993).

Dimensionality Reduction

The task of reducing the number of random variables under consideration. Examples include Principal Component Analysis (PCA) and t-Distributed Stochastic Neighbor Embedding (t-SNE) (Pearson 1901; Maaten and G. Hinton 2008).

Reinforcement Learning

Reinforcement learning involves training a model to make a sequence of decisions by interacting with an environment. The model, or agent, learns to achieve a goal by receiving rewards or penalties based on its actions. Reinforcement learning is commonly used for tasks such as game playing, robotics, and autonomous driving (Sutton and Barto 2018).

Agent

The learner or decision-maker.

Environment

The external system with which the agent interacts.

Action

The set of all possible moves the agent can make.

State

A representation of the current situation of the agent.

Reward

Feedback from the environment based on the agent's actions.

Key Algorithms in Machine Learning

Machine learning encompasses a wide range of algorithms, each suited to different types of tasks and data. This section highlights some of the most important and widely used algorithms in supervised, unsupervised, and reinforcement learning (Alpaydin 2020).

Supervised Learning Algorithms

Linear Regression

Linear regression is a simple yet powerful algorithm used for predicting a continuous target variable based on one or more input features. The goal is to find the best-fitting line that minimizes the difference between the predicted and actual values (Seber and Lee 2012).

$$y = \beta_0 + \beta_1 x_1 + \beta_2 x_2 + \cdots + \beta_n x_n + \epsilon$$

Where y is the target variable, x_i are the input features, β_i are the coefficients, and ϵ is the error term.

Logistic Regression

Logistic regression is used for binary classification tasks, where the goal is to predict one of two possible outcomes. It models the probability that a given input belongs to a particular class using the logistic function (Hosmer, Lemeshow, and Sturdivant 2013).

$$P(y = 1|x) = \frac{1}{1 + e^{-(\beta_0 + \beta_1 x_1 + \beta_2 x_2 + \cdots + \beta_n x_n)}}$$

Where $P(y = 1|x)$ is the probability of the positive class.

Decision Trees

Decision trees are versatile algorithms used for both classification and regression tasks. They split the data into subsets based on the value of input features, creating a tree-like structure where each node represents a decision rule (Quinlan 1986).

Classification and Regression Trees (CART): A popular implementation of decision trees used for classification and regression (Breiman et al. 1984).

Support Vector Machines (SVM)

SVMs are powerful classification algorithms that find the optimal hyperplane that separates the data into different classes. For non-linearly separable data, SVMs use kernel functions to transform the data into a higher-dimensional space where it becomes linearly separable (Cortes and Vapnik 1995).

k-Nearest Neighbors (k-NN)

The k-NN algorithm is a simple, non-parametric method used for classification and regression. It assigns a label to a new data point based on the majority label of its k nearest neighbors in the training set (Cover and Hart 1967).

Unsupervised Learning Algorithms

k-Means Clustering

k-Means is a popular clustering algorithm that partitions the data into k clusters, where each data point belongs to the cluster with the nearest mean. The algorithm iteratively updates the cluster centers until convergence (Lloyd 1982).

Hierarchical Clustering

Hierarchical clustering builds a hierarchy of clusters by either merging smaller clusters into larger ones (agglomerative) or splitting larger clusters into smaller ones (divisive). The result is a dendrogram that represents the nested structure of the data (Murtagh and Legendre 2014).

Principal Component Analysis (PCA)

PCA is a dimensionality reduction technique that transforms the data into a lower-dimensional space by identifying the principal components, which are the directions of maximum variance. PCA helps in visualizing high-dimensional data and reducing computational complexity (Jolliffe 2011).

t-Distributed Stochastic Neighbor Embedding (t-SNE)

t-SNE is a non-linear dimensionality reduction technique used for visualizing high-dimensional data in a low-dimensional space. It is particularly effective for creating visual representations of complex datasets such as images and word embeddings (Maaten and G. Hinton 2008).

Reinforcement Learning Algorithms

Q-Learning

Q-Learning is a model-free reinforcement learning algorithm that learns the optimal action-selection policy by estimating the expected utility (Q-value) of state-action pairs. The agent updates its Q-values based on the rewards received from the environment (Watkins and Dayan 1992).

$$Q(sa) \leftarrow Q(sa) + \alpha[r + \gamma \max_{a'} Q(s'a') - Q(sa)]$$

Where $Q(sa)$ is the Q-value for state s and action a, α is the learning rate, r is the reward, γ is the discount factor, and s' is the next state.

Deep Q-Networks (DQN)

DQNs extend Q-Learning by using deep neural networks to approximate the Q-values. This approach enables the agent to handle high-dimensional state spaces, such as images in video games. DQNs have achieved remarkable success in various tasks, including playing Atari games (Mnih et al. 2015).

Policy Gradient Methods

Policy gradient methods directly optimize the policy, which is the mapping from states to actions, by adjusting the parameters of a neural network. These methods are suitable for continuous action spaces and have been used in applications such as robotics and control systems (Sutton and Barto 2018).

REINFORCE: A basic policy gradient algorithm that updates the policy based on the rewards obtained from sampled trajectories (Ronald J Williams 1992).

Actor-Critic: A hybrid approach that combines value-based and policy-based methods by using an actor to select actions and a critic to estimate the value function (Konda and Tsitsiklis 2000).

Training Machine Learning Models

Training a machine learning model involves several key steps: data collection, data preprocessing, model selection, training, evaluation, and deployment. Each step is crucial for building effective and reliable models (Mohri, Rostamizadeh, and Talwalkar 2018).

Data Collection

The quality and quantity of data play a critical role in the success of machine learning models. Data can be collected from various sources, including databases, sensors, APIs, and web scraping. Ensuring that the data is representative of the problem domain is essential for training robust models (Provost and Fawcett 2013).

Data Preprocessing

Raw data often contains noise, missing values, and inconsistencies that need to be addressed before training a model. Data preprocessing involves several steps (Kotsiantis, Kanellopoulos, and Pintelas 2006):

Cleaning: Removing or imputing missing values and correcting errors.

Normalization: Scaling numerical features to a standard range, such as [0, 1], to ensure that all features contribute equally to the model.

Encoding: Converting categorical features into numerical representations using techniques such as one-hot encoding or label encoding.

Splitting: Dividing the data into training, validation, and test sets to evaluate the model's performance.

Model Selection

Selecting the appropriate model depends on the nature of the problem, the type of data, and the desired performance criteria. Factors to consider include model complexity, interpretability, and computational requirements. Commonly used models include linear regression, decision trees, support vector machines, and neural networks (Domingos 2012).

Training

Training involves optimizing the model's parameters to minimize a loss function that quantifies the difference between the predicted and actual values. This process typically involves iterating through the training data, updating the model parameters using optimization algorithms such as gradient descent (I. Goodfellow, Y. Bengio, and Courville 2016).

Loss Function: A mathematical function that measures the model's prediction error. Examples include mean squared error for regression and cross-entropy loss for classification (Murphy 2012).

Optimization: Techniques such as stochastic gradient descent (SGD) and Adam are used to update the model parameters iteratively to minimize the loss function (Kingma and Ba 2014).

$$\theta \leftarrow \theta - \alpha \nabla_\theta L$$

Where θ represents the weights and biases, α is the learning rate, and L is the loss function.

Evaluation

Evaluating a model's performance is crucial for understanding its strengths and weaknesses. Common evaluation metrics include accuracy, precision, recall, F1-score, and area under the receiver operating characteristic curve (AUC-ROC). Cross-validation is a technique used to assess model performance by splitting the data into multiple subsets and training the model on different combinations of these subsets (Hastie, Tibshirani, and Friedman 2009a).

Deployment

Once a model is trained and evaluated, it can be deployed to make predictions on new, unseen data. Deployment involves integrating the model into a production environment, ensuring that it can handle real-time data and scale to meet user demands. Monitoring the model's performance and updating it with new data are essential for maintaining its accuracy and reliability (Friedman, Hastie, and Tibshirani 2001).

Challenges and Considerations in Machine Learning

While machine learning offers powerful tools for data analysis and prediction, it also presents several challenges and considerations that must be addressed to ensure successful implementation.

Overfitting and Underfitting

Overfitting: Occurs when a model learns the training data too well, capturing noise and outliers, resulting in poor generalization to new data. Techniques such as regularization, dropout, and cross-validation can help mitigate overfitting (I. Goodfellow, Y. Bengio, and Courville 2016).

Underfitting: Occurs when a model is too simple to capture the underlying patterns in the data, leading to poor performance on both training and test data. Increasing model complexity and providing more training data can help address underfitting (Hastie, Tibshirani, and Friedman 2009a).

Bias and Variance

Bias: Refers to the error introduced by approximating a real-world problem with a simplified model. High bias can lead to underfitting (Geman, Bienenstock, and Doursat 1992).

Variance: Refers to the error introduced by the model's sensitivity to small fluctuations in the training data. High variance can lead to overfitting (Geman, Bienenstock, and Doursat 1992).

Bias-Variance Tradeoff: The balance between bias and variance is crucial for building effective models. Techniques such as ensemble learning and cross-validation can help achieve this balance (Breiman 2001).

Interpretability and Explainability

As machine learning models become more complex, interpreting and explaining their decisions becomes increasingly challenging. Ensuring that models are interpretable and their predictions are explainable is important for building trust and accountability, especially in high-stakes applications such as healthcare and finance (Gilpin et al. 2018).

Ethical and Fairness Considerations

Machine learning models can inadvertently learn and perpetuate biases present in the training data. Ensuring fairness and mitigating bias in AI systems is essential for promoting ethical and equitable outcomes. Techniques such as fairness-aware machine learning, bias detection, and mitigation strategies are critical for addressing these concerns (Barocas, Hardt, and Narayanan 2017).

Scalability and Efficiency

Deploying machine learning models in production environments requires scalability and efficiency. Ensuring that models can handle large-scale data and real-time predictions involves optimizing computational resources, parallel processing, and leveraging cloud-based solutions (Geron 2019).

Building a Solid Foundation

Understanding the fundamentals of machine learning is essential for delving into more advanced topics such as Generative AI. By grasping the basic principles, key algorithms, and essential techniques, you are well-equipped to explore the exciting world of AI and harness its potential for innovation and creativity. As we move forward, the knowledge gained in this chapter will serve as a solid foundation for building and understanding complex generative models that push the boundaries of what is possible in artificial intelligence.

Chapter 3

Understanding Neural Networks and Deep Learning

The Brain-Inspired Revolution

Neural networks, inspired by the human brain's structure and function, are the building blocks of modern artificial intelligence. These computational models have revolutionized the field by enabling machines to learn complex patterns and perform tasks that were once considered exclusive to human intelligence. This chapter delves into the architecture, functioning, and training of neural networks, leading to an in-depth understanding of deep learning—a subfield of machine learning that utilizes deep neural networks to achieve remarkable performance across various domains (LeCun, Y. Bengio, and G. Hinton 2015).

The Biological Inspiration: Neurons and Synapses

To understand neural networks, it is essential to appreciate their biological inspiration. The human brain consists of billions of neurons interconnected by synapses. Each neuron receives input signals from other neurons, processes these signals, and transmits the output to other neurons. This intricate network allows the brain to perform complex tasks such as perception, cognition, and decision-making (Kandel, Schwartz, and Jessell 2000).

In an artificial neural network, neurons are represented as nodes, and synapses are represented as weighted connections between these nodes. These weights determine the strength and direction of the signal transmitted between neurons, enabling the network to learn and adapt based on the input data (Haykin 1994).

The Basic Unit: Artificial Neurons

Artificial neurons, also known as perceptrons, are the fundamental units of a neural network. A perceptron receives multiple input signals, applies a weight to each input, sums the weighted inputs, and passes the result through an activation function to produce the output (Rosenblatt 1958). Mathematically, a perceptron can be represented as follows:

$$y = f\left(\sum_{i=1}^{n} w_i x_i + b\right)$$

Where y is the output, x_i are the inputs, w_i are the weights, b is the bias, and f is the activation function.

Activation Functions: Introducing Non-Linearity

Activation functions introduce non-linearity into the network, enabling it to learn complex patterns. Common activation functions include:

Sigmoid Function: Maps the input to a value between 0 and 1.

$$\sigma(x) = \frac{1}{1 + e^{-x}}$$

Hyperbolic Tangent (Tanh) Function: Maps the input to a value between -1 and 1.

$$\tanh(x) = \frac{e^x - e^{-x}}{e^x + e^{-x}}$$

Rectified Linear Unit (ReLU) Function: Maps the input to 0 if it is negative and leaves it unchanged if it is positive.

$$\text{ReLU}(x) = \max(0, x)$$

ReLU is widely used in deep learning due to its simplicity and effectiveness in mitigating the vanishing gradient problem, which occurs when gradients become too small during training, hindering the network's learning process (Nair and Geoffrey E Hinton 2010).

The Architecture of Neural Networks

Neural networks consist of multiple layers of neurons: the input layer, hidden layers, and the output layer. The architecture of a neural network determines its capacity to learn and represent complex functions (LeCun, Y. Bengio, and G. Hinton 2015).

Input Layer: Receives the raw input data.

Hidden Layers: Consist of multiple layers of neurons that process and transform the input data through weighted connections and activation functions. The depth (number of hidden layers) and width (number of neurons per layer) of the network are crucial design parameters.

Output Layer: Produces the final predictions or classifications based on the processed data.

Feedforward Neural Networks

Feedforward neural networks, also known as multi-layer perceptrons (MLPs), are the simplest type of neural network. In these networks, information flows unidirectionally from the input layer to the output layer through the hidden layers. Feedforward networks are suitable for tasks such as classification and regression (I. Goodfellow, Y. Bengio, and Courville 2016).

Convolutional Neural Networks (CNNs)

Convolutional neural networks (CNNs) are designed to process data with a grid-like topology, such as images. CNNs use convolutional layers that apply filters to the input data to extract local features, followed by pooling layers that downsample the feature maps to reduce dimensionality (LeCun, Leon Bottou, et al. 1998).

Convolutional Layers: Apply learnable filters (kernels) to the input data, producing feature maps that capture local patterns.

$$\text{Feature map} = f(\text{Input} * \text{Kernel} + b)$$

Pooling Layers: Perform downsampling operations, such as max pooling or average pooling, to reduce the spatial dimensions of the feature maps.

$$\text{Pooled map} = \text{Pooling}(\text{Feature map})$$

CNNs have achieved state-of-the-art performance in image recognition, object detection, and other computer vision tasks (Krizhevsky, Sutskever, and Geoffrey E. Hinton 2012).

Recurrent Neural Networks (RNNs)

Recurrent neural networks (RNNs) are designed to handle sequential data, such as time series, text, and speech. RNNs have connections that loop back, allowing them to maintain a hidden state that captures information from previous time steps (Hochreiter and Schmidhuber 1997).

Hidden State: Represents the memory of the network, updated at each time step based on the current input and the previous hidden

state.
$$h_t = f(W_h h_{t-1} + W_x x_t + b)$$

Output: Produced at each time step based on the current hidden state.
$$y_t = f(W_y h_t + b)$$

However, RNNs suffer from the vanishing gradient problem, making it difficult to learn long-term dependencies. To address this, advanced architectures such as Long Short-Term Memory (LSTM) and Gated Recurrent Units (GRUs) were developed (Hochreiter and Schmidhuber 1997; K. Cho et al. 2014).

Training Neural Networks

Training a neural network involves optimizing its weights and biases to minimize a loss function that quantifies the difference between the predicted and actual values. The training process typically involves the following steps (I. Goodfellow, Y. Bengio, and Courville 2016):

Forward Propagation

During forward propagation, the input data is passed through the network layer by layer to produce the output. At each layer, the input is transformed by applying weights, biases, and activation functions.

Loss Calculation

The loss function measures the error between the predicted output and the actual target. Common loss functions include mean squared error for regression and cross-entropy loss for classification (I. Goodfellow, Y. Bengio, and Courville 2016).

Backward Propagation

Backward propagation, or backpropagation, calculates the gradients of the loss function with respect to the network's weights and biases.

This process involves applying the chain rule to propagate the error backward through the network from the output layer to the input layer (Rumelhart, Geoffrey E. Hinton, and Ronald J. Williams 1986).

Weight Update

The network's weights and biases are updated using an optimization algorithm such as stochastic gradient descent (SGD) or Adam. These algorithms adjust the parameters in the direction that minimizes the loss function (Kingma and Ba 2014).

$$\theta \leftarrow \theta - \alpha \nabla_\theta L$$

Where θ represents the weights and biases, α is the learning rate, and L is the loss function.

Deep Learning: Extending Neural Networks

Deep learning extends the concepts of neural networks by using architectures with many hidden layers, known as deep neural networks (DNNs). The depth of these networks allows them to learn hierarchical representations of the data, capturing intricate patterns and relationships (LeCun, Y. Bengio, and G. Hinton 2015).

The Importance of Depth

The depth of a neural network determines its capacity to model complex functions. Shallow networks with few hidden layers may struggle to learn intricate patterns, while deep networks can capture multiple levels of abstraction, making them well-suited for tasks such as image recognition and natural language processing (Y. Bengio 2009).

Regularization Techniques

Training deep neural networks involves addressing challenges such as overfitting, where the model performs well on the training data but poorly on new, unseen data. Regularization techniques help mitigate overfitting by adding constraints to the model's parameters or by modifying the training process (Srivastava et al. 2014).

L2 Regularization: Adds a penalty term to the loss function based on the sum of the squared weights.

$$L_{reg} = L + \lambda \sum_i w_i^2$$

Dropout: Randomly drops a fraction of the neurons during training, forcing the network to learn redundant representations.

$$y = f(\text{Dropout}(x))$$

Batch Normalization: Normalizes the inputs of each layer to have zero mean and unit variance, improving training stability and convergence.

$$\hat{x} = \frac{x - \mu}{\sqrt{\sigma^2 + \epsilon}}$$

Transfer Learning

Transfer learning leverages pre-trained models to improve performance on related tasks with limited data. By fine-tuning a pre-trained model on a new dataset, transfer learning enables the reuse of learned features, reducing the need for extensive training data and computational resources (Yosinski et al. 2014).

Popular Deep Learning Frameworks

Several deep learning frameworks have been developed to facilitate the design, training, and deployment of neural networks. These frameworks provide high-level APIs, pre-built modules, and optimization tools, making it easier for researchers and practitioners to implement deep learning models (Abadi et al. 2016).

TensorFlow: Developed by Google, TensorFlow is an open-source framework that supports a wide range of machine learning and deep learning applications. It provides tools for building and training neural networks, as well as for deploying models in production environments (Abadi et al. 2016).

PyTorch: Developed by Facebook, PyTorch is known for its dynamic computation graph and ease of use. It has gained popularity in both research and industry for its flexibility and efficiency in building and training deep learning models (Paszke et al. 2019).

Keras: An open-source neural network library that runs on top of TensorFlow. Keras offers a user-friendly API for quickly prototyping and building deep learning models (Chollet et al. 2015).

Advanced Neural Network Architectures

The field of deep learning continues to evolve, with researchers developing new architectures to tackle increasingly complex tasks. Some of the advanced neural network architectures include:

ResNet (Residual Networks): Introduced by Kaiming He and colleagues, ResNet addresses the problem of vanishing gradients in very deep networks by introducing skip connections, which allow gradients to flow directly through the network.

$$y = f(x) + x$$

(He et al. 2016)

Transformer: Introduced by Vaswani et al., the Transformer architecture revolutionized natural language processing by using self-attention mechanisms to capture long-range dependencies in sequential data. Transformers have become the foundation for state-of-the-art models like BERT and GPT.

$$\text{Attention}(Q, K, V) = \text{softmax}\left(\frac{QK^T}{\sqrt{d_k}}\right) V$$

(Vaswani et al. 2017)

GANs (Generative Adversarial Networks): As discussed in Chapter 1, GANs consist of a generator and a discriminator that are trained simultaneously in a competitive setting, enabling the generation of realistic synthetic data (I. Goodfellow, Pouget-Abadie, et al. 2014).

Applications of Deep Learning

Deep learning has achieved remarkable success across various domains, transforming industries and enabling new applications. Some of the key areas where deep learning has made a significant impact include:

Computer Vision: Deep learning models have achieved state-of-the-art performance in tasks such as image recognition, object detection, and image segmentation. Applications include facial recognition, autonomous driving, and medical imaging (Krizhevsky, Sutskever, and Geoffrey E. Hinton 2012).

Natural Language Processing (NLP): Deep learning has revolutionized NLP, enabling advancements in machine translation, sentiment analysis, and text generation. Models like BERT and GPT have set new benchmarks in language understanding and generation (Devlin et al. 2018; Radford, Wu, et al. 2019).

Speech Recognition: Deep learning models have significantly improved the accuracy of speech recognition systems, enabling applications such as virtual assistants, transcription services, and voice-controlled devices (Graves, A.-r. Mohamed, and G. Hinton 2013).

Recommender Systems: Deep learning is used to build sophisticated recommender systems that provide personalized content recommendations in platforms like Netflix, Amazon, and YouTube (Covington, Adams, and Sargin 2016).

Challenges and Future Directions

While deep learning has achieved impressive results, it also presents several challenges that need to be addressed to unlock its full potential. Some of the key challenges and future directions in deep learning research include:

Interpretability and Explainability: As deep learning models become more complex, understanding their decision-making processes becomes increasingly challenging. Developing methods to interpret and explain model predictions is crucial for building trust and accountability (Lipton 2018).

Data Efficiency: Training deep learning models often requires large amounts of labeled data. Research in data-efficient learning, such as few-shot learning and unsupervised learning, aims to reduce the dependence on extensive labeled datasets (Wang et al. 2020).

Robustness and Security: Ensuring the robustness and security of deep learning models against adversarial attacks and perturbations is critical for deploying models in real-world applications (I. J. Goodfellow, Shlens, and Szegedy 2014).

Scalability: Developing scalable algorithms and architectures that can handle massive datasets and complex tasks efficiently remains an ongoing challenge (Jeff Dean et al. 2012).

The Power of Deep Learning

Neural networks and deep learning have revolutionized the field of artificial intelligence, enabling machines to learn and perform tasks that were once thought to be the exclusive domain of humans. By understanding the architecture, functioning, and training of neural networks, we gain insights into the power and potential of deep learning. As we continue to explore and innovate in this field, the applications and impact of deep learning will only continue to grow, shaping the future of technology and society.

Chapter 4

Generative Models and Their Types

The Creative Machines

Generative models are the backbone of Generative AI, driving the creation of new data that mirrors real-world data in its complexity and diversity. Unlike traditional predictive models that focus on classification or regression, generative models aim to understand and recreate the underlying distribution of data. This chapter explores the various types of generative models, including Generative Adversarial Networks (GANs), Variational Autoencoders (VAEs), and autoregressive models. We will delve into their architectures, mechanisms, and applications, highlighting their contributions to the field of artificial intelligence (I. Goodfellow, Y. Bengio, and Courville 2016).

Understanding Generative Models

Generative models learn the probability distribution of a dataset and can generate new data points that are similar to those in the training set. These models have a wide range of applications, from generating realistic images and videos to synthesizing text and music. The key to their success lies in their ability to capture the complex dependencies and patterns within the data (Kingma and Welling 2019).

Types of Generative Models

Generative models can be categorized based on their underlying mechanisms and architectures. The main types include:

- **Generative Adversarial Networks (GANs)**

- **Variational Autoencoders (VAEs)**

- **Autoregressive Models**

- **Flow-based Models**

- **Energy-based Models**

Generative Adversarial Networks (GANs)

Introduction to GANs

Generative Adversarial Networks (GANs), introduced by (I. Goodfellow, Pouget-Abadie, et al. 2014), have become one of the most influential and widely used generative models. GANs consist of two neural networks: a generator and a discriminator, which are trained simultaneously in a competitive setting.

Generator: The generator creates synthetic data that mimics the real data. It starts with random noise and transforms it into data that resembles the training set.

Discriminator: The discriminator evaluates the authenticity of the data, distinguishing between real and fake data. It outputs a probability indicating whether the input data is real or generated.

The Adversarial Training Process

The training process of GANs is an adversarial game where the generator and discriminator are pitted against each other. The generator aims to produce data that can fool the discriminator, while the discriminator strives to accurately distinguish between real and fake data. This process can be formalized as a minimax optimization problem (I. Goodfellow, Pouget-Abadie, et al. 2014):

$$\min_G \max_D V(D, G) = \mathbb{E}_{x \sim p_{data}(x)}[\log D(x)] + \mathbb{E}_{z \sim p_z(z)}[\log(1 - D(G(z)))]$$

Where $D(x)$ is the discriminator's estimate of the probability that real data x is real and $G(z)$ is the generator's output from random noise z.

Architectural Variants of GANs

Since their inception, various architectural variants of GANs have been developed to improve their performance and stability:

DCGAN (Deep Convolutional GAN): Uses convolutional layers in the generator and discriminator, enhancing the model's ability to handle image data (Radford, Metz, and Chintala 2015).

WGAN (Wasserstein GAN): Introduces the Wasserstein distance as a more stable and interpretable loss function, improving the training of GANs (Arjovsky, Chintala, and Léon Bottou 2017).

StyleGAN: Allows control over the style and features of the generated images, enabling the creation of high-quality and diverse images (Karras, Laine, and Aila 2019).

CycleGAN: Enables unpaired image-to-image translation by learning to translate images from one domain to another without paired examples (Zhu et al. 2017).

Applications of GANs

GANs have been applied in numerous fields, showcasing their versatility and power:

Image Generation: GANs can generate high-resolution and photorealistic images, creating synthetic faces, landscapes, and artwork (Karras, Laine, and Aila 2019).

Data Augmentation: GANs augment training datasets by generating additional data, improving the performance of machine learning models (Antoniou, Storkey, and Edwards 2017).

Image-to-Image Translation: GANs can translate images from one domain to another, such as converting sketches to photos or daytime images to nighttime images (Isola et al. 2017).

Video Generation: GANs are used to create realistic videos and animations, enabling applications in entertainment and virtual reality (Vondrick, Pirsiavash, and Torralba 2016).

Variational Autoencoders (VAEs)

Introduction to VAEs

Variational Autoencoders (VAEs), introduced by (Kingma and Welling 2013), are probabilistic generative models that learn to encode data into a latent space and decode it back to the original space. VAEs combine the principles of autoencoders with variational inference, enabling the generation of new data points by sampling from the latent space.

The VAE Architecture

A VAE consists of two main components:

Encoder: Maps the input data to a latent space by learning the parameters of a probability distribution (typically a Gaussian distribution). The encoder outputs the mean (μ) and standard deviation (σ) of the latent variables.

Decoder: Reconstructs the input data from the sampled latent variables. The decoder generates data that resembles the original input.

Variational Inference

The training of VAEs involves maximizing the evidence lower bound (ELBO), which consists of a reconstruction term and a regularization term (Kingma and Welling 2013):

$$\mathcal{L} = \mathbb{E}_{q(z|x)}[\log p(x|z)] - D_{KL}(q(z|x)||p(z))$$

Where $q(z|x)$ is the approximate posterior distribution, $p(x|z)$ is the likelihood, and D_{KL} is the Kullback-Leibler divergence between the approximate posterior and the prior distribution.

Applications of VAEs

VAEs have been successfully applied to various tasks, leveraging their ability to learn meaningful latent representations:

Image Generation: VAEs generate realistic images by sampling from the learned latent space, producing new and diverse images (Kingma and Welling 2019).

Data Compression: VAEs compress data into a lower-dimensional latent space, enabling efficient storage and transmission (Tian, Kaneko, and Ogata 2014).

Anomaly Detection: VAEs identify anomalies by comparing the reconstruction error of input data, detecting outliers that deviate from the learned distribution (An and S. Cho 2015).

Representation Learning: VAEs learn compact and interpretable representations of data, facilitating downstream tasks such as clustering and classification (Y. Bengio, Courville, and Vincent 2013).

Autoregressive Models

Introduction to Autoregressive Models

Autoregressive models generate data sequentially, one step at a time, by conditioning each step on the previous steps. These models have been widely used in time series analysis, natural language processing, and other sequential data applications (Graves, A.-r. Mohamed, and G. Hinton 2013).

The Autoregressive Process

In an autoregressive model, the probability of the next data point is conditioned on the previous data points:

$$p(x) = \prod_{t=1}^{T} p(x_t | x_{1:t-1})$$

Where x_t is the data point at time step t and $x_{1:t-1}$ are the previous data points.

Popular Autoregressive Models

Several autoregressive models have been developed for different types of data:

AR (Autoregressive) Models: Used for time series forecasting by modeling the dependency of a value on its previous values (Box et al. 2015).

RNNs (Recurrent Neural Networks): Handle sequential data by maintaining a hidden state that captures information from previous time steps (Graves, A.-r. Mohamed, and G. Hinton 2013).

PixelRNN and PixelCNN: Generate images pixel by pixel, conditioning each pixel on the previously generated pixels (Oord, Kalchbrenner, and Kavukcuoglu 2016).

Transformer-based Models: Utilize self-attention mechanisms to model long-range dependencies in sequential data. Examples include GPT (Generative Pre-trained Transformer) and BERT (Bidirectional Encoder Representations from Transformers) (Vaswani et al. 2017).

Applications of Autoregressive Models

Autoregressive models excel in generating sequential data, with applications spanning various domains:

Time Series Forecasting: Autoregressive models predict future values of time series data, such as stock prices and weather conditions (Box et al. 2015).

Text Generation: Models like GPT generate coherent and contextually relevant text, enabling applications in chatbots, content creation, and translation (Radford, Wu, et al. 2019).

Music Generation: Autoregressive models compose music by generating sequences of notes and rhythms, creating original compositions (Briot, Hadjeres, and Pachet 2020).

Speech Synthesis: Models like WaveNet generate high-quality speech waveforms, improving text-to-speech systems (Oord, Dieleman, et al. 2016).

Flow-based Models

Introduction to Flow-based Models

Flow-based models are generative models that learn the data distribution by transforming a simple base distribution (e.g., Gaussian) into the target distribution using invertible transformations. These models offer exact likelihood estimation and efficient sampling, making them powerful tools for generative tasks (Dinh, Sohl-Dickstein, and S. Bengio 2016).

The Flow-based Process

Flow-based models use a series of invertible transformations f to map the input data x to a latent variable z:

$$z = f(x)$$

The likelihood of the data can be computed using the change of variables formula (Dinh, Sohl-Dickstein, and S. Bengio 2016):

$$p(x) = p(z) \left| \det \frac{\partial f}{\partial x} \right|$$

Where $p(z)$ is the base distribution and $\left| \det \frac{\partial f}{\partial x} \right|$ is the determinant of the Jacobian matrix of the transformation f.

Popular Flow-based Models

Several flow-based models have been developed to handle different types of data:

RealNVP (Real-valued Non-Volume Preserving): Uses affine coupling layers to ensure invertibility and efficient computation of the Jacobian determinant (Dinh, Sohl-Dickstein, and S. Bengio 2016).

Glow: Extends RealNVP with additional features like multi-scale architecture and 1x1 invertible convolutions, improving the quality of generated images (Kingma and Dhariwal 2018).

Normalizing Flows: A general framework for constructing complex distributions by composing multiple invertible transformations (Rezende and S. Mohamed 2015).

Applications of Flow-based Models

Flow-based models have been applied to various generative tasks, leveraging their ability to model complex distributions:

Image Generation: Flow-based models generate high-quality images with exact likelihood estimation, providing insights into the learned distribution (Kingma and Dhariwal 2018).

Density Estimation: These models estimate the density of high-dimensional data, enabling applications in anomaly detection and data compression (Rezende and S. Mohamed 2015).

Latent Variable Modeling: Flow-based models learn expressive latent representations, facilitating downstream tasks such as clustering and interpolation (Dinh, Sohl-Dickstein, and S. Bengio 2016).

Energy-based Models

Introduction to Energy-based Models

Energy-based models (EBMs) define an energy function that assigns a scalar energy value to each configuration of the input data. The model learns to assign low energy to real data and high energy to improbable data. EBMs offer a flexible framework for modeling complex distributions, though they can be challenging to train (LeCun, F. J. Huang, and Léon Bottou 2006).

The Energy-based Process

In EBMs, the energy function $E(x)$ is used to define the probability distribution of the data (LeCun, F. J. Huang, and Léon Bottou 2006):

$$p(x) = \frac{e^{-E(x)}}{Z}$$

Where Z is the partition function, ensuring that the distribution sums to one.

Training Energy-based Models

Training EBMs involves minimizing the energy of the real data while maximizing the energy of the generated data. This process can be formalized as (LeCun, F. J. Huang, and Léon Bottou 2006):

$$\mathcal{L} = \mathbb{E}_{x \sim p_{data}(x)}[E(x)] - \mathbb{E}_{x \sim p_{model}(x)}[E(x)]$$

However, computing the partition function Z and sampling from the model distribution $p_{model}(x)$ can be computationally intensive.

Applications of Energy-based Models

EBMs have been applied to various tasks, though their use is less widespread due to training challenges:

Image Generation: EBMs generate images by sampling from the learned energy distribution, though this process can be slow and computationally demanding (LeCun, F. J. Huang, and Léon Bottou 2006).

Anomaly Detection: EBMs detect anomalies by evaluating the energy of input data, identifying outliers with high energy values (LeCun, F. J. Huang, and Léon Bottou 2006).

Representation Learning: EBMs learn meaningful representations by minimizing the energy of real data, facilitating tasks such as clustering and classification (LeCun, F. J. Huang, and Léon Bottou 2006).

The Diversity of Generative Models

Generative models encompass a diverse range of architectures and mechanisms, each with its strengths and applications. From the adversarial training of GANs to the probabilistic framework of VAEs and the sequential generation of autoregressive models, these models have transformed the landscape of artificial intelligence. Understanding the principles and applications of these generative models is crucial for harnessing their potential and advancing the field of Generative AI.

Chapter 5

Applications of Generative AI

Transforming Industries and Society

Generative AI is reshaping various industries and aspects of society by enabling machines to create and innovate in ways that were once thought impossible. From art and entertainment to healthcare and education, the applications of Generative AI are vast and diverse. This chapter explores some of the most impactful and promising applications of Generative AI, showcasing how this technology is driving innovation and transforming our world.

Generative AI in Art and Creativity

Generative AI is revolutionizing the field of art and creativity by providing artists with new tools and methods to explore their artistic expression. AI-generated art has gained recognition and acceptance, challenging traditional notions of creativity and authorship.

AI-Generated Art

Artists are collaborating with AI to create unique pieces that blend human creativity with machine-generated patterns. Generative models can analyze existing artworks and produce new pieces that reflect similar styles, opening up new possibilities for artistic expression (Elgammal et al. 2017).

Case Study: Portrait of Edmond de Belamy In 2018, the AI-generated artwork "Portrait of Edmond de Belamy," created by the Paris-based art collective Obvious, was sold at Christie's auction for $432,500. The portrait was generated using a Generative Adversarial Network (GAN), highlighting the potential of AI in the art world (Christie's 2018).

Music Composition

Generative AI is being used to compose original music, assist musicians in the creative process, and generate soundtracks for various applications. AI models can analyze vast collections of music and learn to generate compositions in various styles and genres (Briot, Hadjeres, and Pachet 2020).

Case Study: OpenAI's MuseNet OpenAI's MuseNet is a deep neural network that can generate music with ten different instruments and in a variety of styles, from classical to pop. MuseNet demonstrates the potential of Generative AI to create complex and harmonious musical compositions (Dhariwal et al. 2020).

Fashion and Design

Generative AI is transforming the fashion and design industry by enabling the creation of innovative designs and personalized fashion. AI models can generate new clothing designs, suggest fashion trends, and even create virtual fashion shows (Mukherjee, Banerjee, and Garg 2020).

Case Study: Project Muze Project Muze, a collaboration between Google and the fashion platform Zalando, uses Generative AI to create personalized fashion designs based on user preferences and current fashion trends. The project showcases how AI can be used to enhance creativity in fashion design (Google and Zalando 2016).

Generative AI in Healthcare

Generative AI is making significant contributions to the healthcare industry by improving diagnostics, drug discovery, and personalized treatment plans. The ability to generate realistic medical data and predict outcomes is revolutionizing healthcare delivery.

Medical Imaging

Generative AI models can enhance medical imaging by generating high-resolution images from low-quality inputs, improving the accuracy of diagnostic tools. These models can also help in detecting anomalies and predicting disease progression (Frid-Adar et al. 2018).

Case Study: NVIDIA's GAN-based Medical Imaging NVIDIA has developed GAN-based models that can generate high-quality medical images, such as MRI scans, from limited data. These models improve the diagnostic process by providing clearer images and reducing the need for invasive procedures (Alarcon 2018).

Drug Discovery

Generative AI is accelerating the drug discovery process by predicting the properties of new compounds and suggesting potential drug candidates. AI models can analyze vast datasets of chemical compounds and generate new molecules with desired properties (Zhavoronkov et al. 2019).

Case Study: Insilico Medicine Insilico Medicine uses Generative AI to design novel drug candidates for various diseases. Their AI-driven platform has successfully identified potential compounds for diseases such as cancer and fibrosis, demonstrating the potential of AI in drug discovery (Medicine 2023).

Personalized Medicine

Generative AI can analyze patient data to create personalized treatment plans, predict treatment outcomes, and identify potential side effects. This approach enhances the precision and effectiveness of medical treatments (Miotto et al. 2017).

Case Study: IBM Watson for Oncology IBM Watson for Oncology uses AI to analyze patient medical records and generate personalized treatment recommendations for cancer patients. The system leverages vast amounts of medical literature and clinical data to provide evidence-based treatment options (Nature 2024).

Generative AI in Education

Generative AI is transforming education by enabling personalized learning experiences, automating content creation, and enhancing educational tools. AI-driven applications are helping educators and students achieve better learning outcomes.

Personalized Learning

Generative AI can create personalized learning pathways for students by analyzing their learning styles, strengths, and weaknesses. AI-driven platforms can adapt educational content to meet the individual needs of each student (Holmes, Bialik, and Fadel 2019).

Case Study: Squirrel AI Squirrel AI, a leading AI-powered education company in China, uses Generative AI to create personalized learning plans for students. The platform analyzes student performance data and generates customized content to help students achieve their learning goals (AI 2019).

Content Creation

Generative AI can automate the creation of educational content, such as quizzes, assignments, and interactive lessons. This automation reduces the workload for educators and ensures that content is tailored to the needs of the students (Tomar 2019).

Case Study: Content Technologies Inc. (CTI) Content Technologies Inc. (CTI) uses AI to generate personalized textbooks and learning materials based on student data. Their AI-driven platform creates dynamic content that adapts to the learning pace and preferences of each student (Sciforce 2023).

Language Learning

Generative AI is being used to develop language learning applications that provide interactive and immersive experiences. AI-driven language tutors can generate realistic dialogues, provide instant feedback, and adapt to the learner's proficiency level (X. Liu, W. Zhang, C. Zhang, et al. 2019).

Case Study: Duolingo's AI-Powered Chatbots Duolingo, a popular language learning app, uses AI-powered chatbots to simulate conversations with learners. The chatbots generate realistic dialogues and provide personalized feedback, enhancing the language learning experience (Duolingo 2023).

Generative AI in Business and Marketing

Generative AI is transforming business and marketing by enabling the creation of personalized content, optimizing marketing strategies, and enhancing customer engagement. AI-driven applications are helping businesses improve their operations and connect with customers in innovative ways.

Content Generation

Generative AI can create personalized marketing content, such as advertisements, social media posts, and email campaigns. AI-driven content generation ensures that marketing messages are tailored to the preferences and behaviors of individual customers.

Case Study: Persado's AI-Powered Copywriting Persado uses AI to generate personalized marketing messages that resonate with customers. Their AI-powered platform analyzes customer data and generates content that maximizes engagement and conversion rates (Persado 2020).

Customer Insights

Generative AI can analyze customer data to generate insights and predict future behaviors. This information helps businesses make informed decisions and develop strategies that meet the needs of their customers.

Case Study: Salesforce's Einstein AI Salesforce's Einstein AI analyzes customer data to provide actionable insights and predictions. The platform helps businesses understand customer preferences, optimize marketing campaigns, and improve customer satisfaction (Salesforce 2023).

Product Design and Development

Generative AI can assist in product design and development by generating new ideas, optimizing designs, and predicting market trends. AI-driven tools enable businesses to innovate and bring products to market faster (Autodesk 2019).

Case Study: Autodesk's Generative Design Autodesk uses Generative AI to create innovative product designs. Their AI-driven platform generates multiple design options based on specified constraints and objectives, allowing designers to explore a wide range of possibilities (Autodesk 2019).

Generative AI in Gaming and Virtual Environments

Generative AI is revolutionizing the gaming industry by creating immersive and dynamic virtual environments. AI-driven applications are enhancing game design, character development, and player experiences.

Procedural Content Generation

Generative AI can create vast and varied game worlds through procedural content generation. This technique allows game developers to generate landscapes, levels, and assets algorithmically, providing players with unique and engaging experiences (Shaker, Togelius, and Nelson 2016).

Case Study: No Man's Sky No Man's Sky, a popular video game, uses procedural content generation to create an expansive universe with billions of unique planets. The game's AI-driven algorithms generate diverse landscapes, flora, and fauna, offering players endless exploration opportunities (H. Games n.d.).

Intelligent NPCs

Generative AI can develop intelligent non-player characters (NPCs) that interact with players in meaningful ways. AI-driven NPCs can adapt to player actions, provide dynamic dialogues, and enhance the overall gaming experience (Booth 2019).

Case Study: Red Dead Redemption 2 Red Dead Redemption 2 features AI-driven NPCs that exhibit realistic behaviors and interactions. The game's NPCs adapt to player actions and provide immersive and engaging experiences, showcasing the potential of Generative AI in game development (R. Games n.d.).

Virtual Reality and Augmented Reality

Generative AI is enhancing virtual reality (VR) and augmented reality (AR) experiences by creating realistic environments and interactions. AI-driven applications enable the creation of dynamic and responsive virtual worlds (Milgram and Kishino 1994).

Case Study: AI-Driven Virtual Reality AI-driven virtual reality is transforming how immersive environments are created and experienced. By leveraging Generative AI, developers can design dynamic and interactive virtual spaces that adapt to user interactions, offering more engaging and realistic experiences. This technology pushes the boundaries of what is possible in virtual reality, creating personalized and evolving environments for users (Crockett 2023).

Generative AI in Finance and Economics

Generative AI is transforming the finance and economics sectors by enabling advanced data analysis, predictive modeling, and automated decision-making. AI-driven applications are helping financial institutions and economists make better-informed decisions and optimize their operations.

Algorithmic Trading

Generative AI is being used to develop sophisticated algorithmic trading systems that analyze market data, identify patterns, and execute trades autonomously. AI-driven trading algorithms can adapt to market conditions and optimize trading strategies (Heaton, Polson, and Witte 2017).

Case Study: Renaissance Technologies Renaissance Technologies, a leading hedge fund, uses AI-driven algorithms to analyze vast amounts of financial data and execute trades. Their AI-powered trading systems have consistently delivered strong performance, demonstrating the potential of Generative AI in finance (Heaton, Polson, and Witte 2017).

Risk Management

Generative AI can help financial institutions identify and mitigate risks by analyzing historical data and generating predictive models. AI-driven risk management systems can detect anomalies, assess credit risk, and optimize investment portfolios (Li et al. 2019).

Case Study: JPMorgan Chase's COiN Platform JPMorgan Chase's COiN platform uses Generative AI to analyze legal documents and extract critical information. The AI-driven system helps the bank manage risks and ensure compliance, reducing the time and effort required for manual reviews (School 2018).

The Impact of Generative AI

Generative AI is revolutionizing various industries and aspects of society by enabling machines to create, innovate, and optimize. The applications explored in this chapter highlight the transformative potential of Generative AI in art, healthcare, education, business, gaming, finance, and more. As technology continues to advance, the impact of Generative AI will only grow, driving innovation and shaping the future of our world.

Chapter 6

Ethical Implications of Generative AI

The Responsibility of Creation

Generative AI holds immense potential to transform various industries and enhance human creativity. However, with great power comes great responsibility. The ability to generate realistic and convincing data—whether images, text, or videos—raises significant ethical concerns. This chapter delves into the ethical implications of Generative AI, exploring issues such as misinformation, privacy, bias, and accountability. Understanding these challenges is crucial for ensuring that Generative AI is developed and deployed responsibly (Floridi et al. 2018).

Misinformation and Deepfakes

One of the most prominent ethical concerns surrounding Generative AI is the creation of deepfakes—synthetic media generated by AI that can convincingly mimic real people. Deepfakes have the potential to spread misinformation, manipulate public opinion, and damage reputations (Chesney and Citron 2019).

What Are Deepfakes?

Deepfakes are highly realistic and manipulated videos or images created using Generative Adversarial Networks (GANs). These technologies can superimpose faces, alter expressions, and create entirely new scenes, making it difficult to distinguish between real and fake content (I. Goodfellow, Pouget-Abadie, et al. 2014).

The Risks of Deepfakes

The ability to create convincing deepfakes poses several risks:

Misinformation: Deepfakes can be used to spread false information, manipulate political events, and deceive the public (Chesney and Citron 2019).

Reputation Damage: Individuals can be falsely portrayed in compromising situations, leading to personal and professional harm.

Trust Erosion: The prevalence of deepfakes can erode trust in digital media and undermine the credibility of legitimate sources.

Mitigating Deepfake Risks

Addressing the risks associated with deepfakes requires a multi-faceted approach:

Detection Technologies: Developing advanced detection algorithms that can identify deepfakes and distinguish them from genuine content (Rössler et al. 2019).

Regulation and Legislation: Implementing policies and regulations that penalize the malicious use of deepfakes and protect individuals' rights (Calo 2017).

Public Awareness: Educating the public about the existence and potential risks of deepfakes, promoting critical thinking and media literacy.

Privacy Concerns

Generative AI can generate realistic data based on personal information, raising significant privacy concerns. The ability to recreate individuals' images, voices, and behaviors without their consent poses ethical dilemmas (Aggarwal and Abdelzaher 2018).

Synthetic Data and Privacy

Generative AI can produce synthetic data that mimics real individuals, raising questions about privacy and consent:

Personal Data Generation: AI models can generate synthetic identities that closely resemble real people, potentially leading to identity theft and privacy breaches (Miotto et al. 2017).

Voice Synthesis: AI-generated voices can mimic individuals, enabling unauthorized use of someone's voice for malicious purposes (C. Zhang et al. 2021).

Protecting Privacy in Generative AI

Ensuring privacy in the context of Generative AI involves several strategies:

Anonymization: Developing techniques to anonymize data before using it to train generative models, reducing the risk of re-identification (El Emam, Mosquera, and Hu 2021).

Consent Mechanisms: Implementing consent mechanisms that allow individuals to control how their data is used and to opt out of generative AI applications (S. Jain and Thakur 2019).

Ethical Guidelines: Establishing ethical guidelines for the development and deployment of generative models, prioritizing privacy and individual rights (Jobin, Ienca, and Vayena 2019).

Bias and Fairness

Generative AI models learn from existing data, which can contain biases and reflect societal inequalities. If not addressed, these biases can be perpetuated and amplified by the AI models (Mehrabi et al. 2021).

Sources of Bias

Bias in generative models can arise from various sources:

Training Data: If the training data contains biases or is not representative, the model will learn and reproduce these biases (Buolamwini and Gebru 2018).

Model Architecture: Certain model architectures may inherently favor certain types of data or decisions, leading to biased outcomes (Olteanu et al. 2019).

Algorithmic Bias: The algorithms used to train and fine-tune generative models can introduce or exacerbate biases (Barocas, Hardt, and Narayanan 2017).

Addressing Bias in Generative AI

Mitigating bias and ensuring fairness in Generative AI requires a proactive approach:

Diverse Datasets: Ensuring that training datasets are diverse and representative of different demographics and perspectives (Binns 2018).

Bias Detection: Developing tools and methodologies to detect and measure bias in generative models, enabling corrective actions (Barocas, Hardt, and Narayanan 2019).

Fairness Metrics: Implementing fairness metrics to evaluate and compare the performance of generative models across different groups (Verma and Rubin 2018).

Inclusive Design: Involving diverse teams in the design and development of generative models to incorporate multiple viewpoints and reduce biases (Raji and Buolamwini 2020).

Accountability and Transparency

As generative models become more complex and influential, ensuring accountability and transparency in their development and deployment is crucial (Doshi-Velez and Kim 2017).

The Black Box Problem

Many generative models, particularly deep learning models, operate as "black boxes," making it difficult to understand how they make decisions and generate data. This lack of transparency can hinder accountability and trust (Rudin 2019).

Ensuring Accountability

To ensure accountability in Generative AI, several measures can be taken:

Explainability: Developing methods to interpret and explain the decisions and outputs of generative models, making their inner workings more transparent (Gilpin et al. 2018).

Auditability: Implementing mechanisms for auditing generative models, tracking their development process, and documenting their decisions and outputs (B. D. Mittelstadt et al. 2016).

Ethical AI Practices: Promoting ethical AI practices that prioritize transparency, accountability, and responsibility in the development and deployment of generative models (Jobin, Ienca, and Vayena 2019).

Ethical Frameworks and Guidelines

Various ethical frameworks and guidelines have been proposed to address the ethical implications of AI, including Generative AI. These frameworks provide principles and best practices for responsible AI development (Floridi et al. 2018).

The Asilomar AI Principles

The Asilomar AI Principles, developed by the Future of Life Institute, provide guidelines for the ethical development of AI, emphasizing safety, transparency, and accountability (Yudkowsky 2008).

The EU Ethics Guidelines for Trustworthy AI

The European Union has developed Ethics Guidelines for Trustworthy AI, which outline key requirements for AI systems, including human agency, privacy, transparency, and non-discrimination (Commission 2019).

The IEEE Global Initiative on Ethics of Autonomous and Intelligent Systems

The IEEE Global Initiative provides ethical guidelines and standards for the design and deployment of autonomous and intelligent systems, promoting transparency, accountability, and fairness (IEEE 2019).

Navigating the Ethical Landscape

The ethical implications of Generative AI are complex and multifaceted, requiring careful consideration and proactive measures to ensure responsible development and deployment. By understanding the potential risks and challenges, we can develop ethical guidelines and frameworks that promote the beneficial use of Generative AI while safeguarding against its potential harms. As we continue to innovate and push the boundaries of what AI can achieve, it is crucial to prioritize ethical considerations and work towards a future where AI serves the greater good.

Chapter 7

Mitigating Bias and Ensuring Fairness

Striving for Equitable AI

As Generative AI continues to evolve and impact various aspects of society, addressing issues of bias and fairness becomes increasingly important. Bias in AI systems can lead to unfair outcomes, perpetuate stereotypes, and exacerbate social inequalities. This chapter explores the sources of bias in Generative AI, strategies for mitigating bias, and approaches to ensuring fairness in AI systems. By promoting fairness and inclusivity, we can harness the full potential of Generative AI while minimizing its negative impact (Mehrabi et al. 2021).

Understanding Bias in AI

Bias in AI systems can arise from various sources, leading to skewed outcomes that may disadvantage certain groups or individuals. Understanding these sources is crucial for developing effective mitigation strategies (Barocas, Hardt, and Narayanan 2019).

Sources of Bias

Training Data Bias: Biases present in the training data can be learned and perpetuated by AI models. This can result from historical inequalities, sampling bias, or unrepresentative datasets (Buolamwini and Gebru 2018).

Algorithmic Bias: The algorithms used to develop and fine-tune AI models can introduce biases. Certain algorithms may favor specific types of data or decisions, leading to biased outcomes (Olteanu et al. 2019).

Human Bias: Biases held by developers, researchers, and stakeholders can influence the design and implementation of AI systems, leading to biased results (Mehrabi et al. 2021).

Types of Bias

Bias in AI can manifest in different forms, affecting various aspects of the system's performance and impact:

Representation Bias: Occurs when certain groups or attributes are underrepresented or misrepresented in the training data, leading to skewed outcomes (Barocas, Hardt, and Narayanan 2019).

Measurement Bias: Arises when the metrics used to evaluate AI performance favor certain groups or attributes over others, leading to biased assessments (Verma and Rubin 2018).

Algorithmic Bias: Results from the inherent biases of the algorithms used in AI models, which may favor specific types of data or decisions (Barocas, Hardt, and Narayanan 2019).

Mitigating Bias in Generative AI

Addressing bias in Generative AI requires a proactive approach that encompasses data collection, model development, and evaluation. Several strategies can help mitigate bias and promote fairness:

Diverse and Representative Datasets

Ensuring that training datasets are diverse and represent various demographics and perspectives is crucial for reducing bias. This involves collecting data from a wide range of sources and ensuring that all relevant groups are adequately represented (Binns 2018).

Bias Detection and Measurement

Developing tools and methodologies to detect and measure bias in AI models is essential for identifying and addressing biases. This includes analyzing the model's performance across different groups and using fairness metrics to evaluate its impact (Verma and Rubin 2018).

Fairness Metrics

Implementing fairness metrics helps evaluate the performance of AI models in terms of equity and inclusivity. Common fairness metrics include:

Demographic Parity: Ensures that the model's decisions are independent of protected attributes, such as race or gender (Mehrabi et al. 2021).

Equalized Odds: Ensures that the model's true positive and false positive rates are equal across different groups (Hardt, Price, and Srebro 2016).

Calibration: Ensures that the model's predicted probabilities are accurate and consistent across different groups (Pleiss et al. 2017).

Bias Mitigation Techniques

Several techniques can help mitigate bias in AI models:

Pre-processing: Involves modifying the training data to reduce bias, such as re-sampling, re-weighting, or anonymizing data (Kamiran and Calders 2012).

In-processing: Involves modifying the training algorithm to reduce bias, such as incorporating fairness constraints or regularization techniques (Zafar et al. 2017).

Post-processing: Involves modifying the model's outputs to reduce bias, such as re-calibrating predictions or applying fairness adjustments (Hardt, Price, and Srebro 2016).

Ensuring Fairness in AI Systems

Promoting fairness in AI systems goes beyond mitigating bias. It involves ensuring that AI systems are designed, developed, and deployed in a manner that respects and promotes equity and inclusivity.

Inclusive Design

Involving diverse teams in the design and development of AI systems helps incorporate multiple viewpoints and reduce biases. This includes engaging stakeholders from different backgrounds and ensuring that their perspectives are considered in the decision-making process (Holstein et al. 2019).

Transparency and Accountability

Ensuring transparency and accountability in AI systems is crucial for building trust and promoting fairness. This involves:

Explainability: Developing methods to interpret and explain the decisions and outputs of AI models, making their inner workings more transparent (Gilpin et al. 2018).

Auditability: Implementing mechanisms for auditing AI systems, tracking their development process, and documenting their decisions and outputs (B. D. Mittelstadt et al. 2016).

Ethical AI Practices: Promoting ethical AI practices that prioritize transparency, accountability, and responsibility in the development and deployment of AI systems (Jobin, Ienca, and Vayena 2019).

Regulation and Legislation

Implementing policies and regulations that promote fairness and equity in AI systems is essential for ensuring their responsible use. This includes:

Fairness Standards: Establishing standards and guidelines for fairness in AI, ensuring that AI systems are designed and deployed in a manner that respects and promotes equity (Barocas, Hardt, and Narayanan 2019).

Accountability Mechanisms: Developing mechanisms to hold developers, researchers, and organizations accountable for the fairness and impact of their AI systems (Danks and London 2017).

Public Awareness and Education: Raising awareness about the importance of fairness in AI and educating the public about their rights and the potential impact of AI systems (Jobin, Ienca, and Vayena 2019).

Building Fair and Inclusive AI

Ensuring fairness in Generative AI is a complex and ongoing challenge that requires a proactive and holistic approach. By understanding the sources and types of bias, implementing effective mitigation strategies, and promoting transparency and accountability, we can build AI systems that are fair, inclusive, and equitable. As we continue to innovate and push the boundaries of what AI can achieve, it is crucial to prioritize fairness and work towards a future where AI serves the greater good.

Chapter 8

Future Trends in Generative AI

The Road Ahead

Generative AI has already made significant strides in various fields, from art and entertainment to healthcare and finance. As the technology continues to evolve, new trends and advancements are emerging, promising to further expand the capabilities and applications of Generative AI. This chapter explores some of the most exciting future trends in Generative AI, including advancements in model architectures, new applications, ethical considerations, and the potential societal impact (LeCun, Y. Bengio, and G. Hinton 2015).

Advancements in Model Architectures

The development of new model architectures and techniques is driving the next wave of innovation in Generative AI. These advancements are enhancing the performance, efficiency, and versatility of generative models.

Transformers and Attention Mechanisms

Transformers and attention mechanisms have revolutionized the field of natural language processing and are now being applied to other domains, such as computer vision and audio processing. The ability of transformers to capture long-range dependencies and handle large datasets makes them a powerful tool for generative tasks (Vaswani et al. 2017).

Vision Transformers (ViTs): Adapt the transformer architecture for image processing tasks, achieving state-of-the-art performance in image classification, segmentation, and generation (Dosovitskiy et al. 2020).

Generative Pre-trained Transformers (GPT): Continue to push the boundaries of text generation, enabling applications such as chatbots, content creation, and translation (Radford, Wu, et al. 2019).

Improved Training Techniques

Advancements in training techniques are helping to overcome some of the challenges associated with generative models, such as mode collapse and training instability (Salimans et al. 2016).

Contrastive Learning: Leverages contrasting pairs of data to learn robust and discriminative features, improving the quality and diversity of generated data (T. Chen et al. 2020).

Self-Supervised Learning: Utilizes large amounts of unlabeled data to pre-train generative models, reducing the reliance on labeled datasets and enhancing model performance (Doersch, Gupta, and Efros 2015).

Hybrid Models

Combining different types of generative models can leverage their complementary strengths and mitigate their weaknesses.

VAE-GAN Hybrids: Combine the generative capabilities of VAEs with the adversarial training of GANs, producing high-quality and diverse outputs (Larsen et al. 2015).

Flow-GAN Hybrids: Integrate the exact likelihood estimation of flow-based models with the adversarial training of GANs, improving both generation quality and interpretability (Grover, Dhar, and Ermon 2018).

New Applications of Generative AI

As generative models become more advanced, new and innovative applications are emerging across various fields.

Drug Discovery and Healthcare

Generative AI is transforming the field of drug discovery by enabling the rapid generation and evaluation of potential drug candidates (Zhavoronkov et al. 2019).

Molecule Generation: Generative models can design novel molecules with desired properties, accelerating the drug discovery process (Segler, Preuss, and Waller 2018).

Medical Imaging: Generative models can enhance medical imaging techniques, improving the quality and accuracy of diagnostic tools (Frid-Adar et al. 2018).

Content Creation and Personalization

Generative AI is revolutionizing content creation by enabling the generation of personalized and high-quality content.

Automated Writing: Generative models can create articles, stories, and marketing content tailored to specific audiences and preferences.

Music Composition: AI-powered music generation tools can compose original pieces, assist musicians in the creative process, and generate personalized soundtracks (Dhariwal et al. 2020).

Gaming and Virtual Worlds

Generative AI is enhancing the gaming industry by enabling the creation of dynamic and immersive virtual environments.

Procedural Content Generation: Generative models can create vast and varied game worlds, characters, and storylines, providing players with unique and engaging experiences (Shaker, Togelius, and Nelson 2016).

Intelligent NPCs: AI-powered non-player characters (NPCs) can interact with players in meaningful ways, enhancing the realism and depth of virtual environments (Booth 2019).

Ethical Considerations and Responsible AI

As Generative AI continues to advance, addressing ethical considerations and promoting responsible AI development is crucial.

Ethical AI Frameworks

Developing and implementing ethical AI frameworks can guide the responsible development and deployment of generative models (Jobin, Ienca, and Vayena 2019).

Transparency and Explainability: Ensuring that generative models are transparent and their decisions are explainable to build trust and accountability (Gilpin et al. 2018).

Fairness and Inclusivity: Promoting fairness and inclusivity in AI systems by addressing bias and ensuring that generative models serve diverse populations (Mehrabi et al. 2021).

Regulation and Governance

Implementing effective regulation and governance mechanisms is essential for managing the societal impact of Generative AI (B. D. Mittelstadt et al. 2016).

Policy Development: Collaborating with policymakers to develop regulations that address the ethical and societal implications of generative models (Danks and London 2017).

AI Governance: Establishing governance structures that oversee the development, deployment, and use of generative models to ensure they align with ethical principles and societal values (Jobin, Ienca, and Vayena 2019).

The Societal Impact of Generative AI

Generative AI has the potential to bring about significant societal changes, both positive and negative. Understanding and managing this impact is crucial for maximizing the benefits and minimizing the risks.

Positive Impact

Generative AI can drive innovation, enhance creativity, and improve quality of life across various domains.

Economic Growth: Generative AI can boost productivity, create new industries, and generate economic opportunities (Brynjolfsson, Rock, and Syverson 2017).

Healthcare Advancements: AI-powered tools can improve healthcare delivery, enhance diagnostic accuracy, and accelerate drug discovery (Topol 2019).

Educational Tools: Generative models can create personalized learning experiences, making education more accessible and effective (Holmes, Bialik, and Fadel 2019).

Negative Impact and Mitigation

Addressing the potential negative impact of Generative AI is crucial for ensuring its responsible use.

Job Displacement: The automation of creative and knowledge-based tasks can lead to job displacement. Developing strategies for workforce transition and reskilling is essential (Brynjolfsson, Rock, and Syverson 2017).

Misinformation and Deepfakes: The misuse of generative models to create deepfakes and spread misinformation poses significant risks. Implementing detection technologies and regulatory measures can help mitigate these risks (Chesney and Citron 2019).

Privacy Concerns: The generation of synthetic data that mimics real individuals raises privacy concerns. Developing privacy-preserving techniques and consent mechanisms is crucial for protecting individuals' rights (I. J. Goodfellow, Shlens, and Szegedy 2014).

Embracing the Future of Generative AI

The future of Generative AI is filled with exciting possibilities and significant challenges. As we continue to push the boundaries of what AI can achieve, it is crucial to prioritize ethical considerations, promote fairness and inclusivity, and ensure responsible development and deployment. By embracing these principles, we can harness the full potential of Generative AI to drive innovation, enhance creativity, and improve quality of life while safeguarding against its potential harms.

Chapter 9

Building Your Own Generative AI Models

From Theory to Practice

Building your own Generative AI models can be a rewarding and insightful experience. Whether you are a researcher, developer, or enthusiast, understanding the practical steps involved in creating generative models is essential. This chapter provides a comprehensive guide to building Generative AI models, covering data collection, model selection, training, and evaluation. We will also explore various tools and frameworks that facilitate the development of generative models (I. Goodfellow, Y. Bengio, and Courville 2016).

Data Collection and Preparation

Data is the foundation of any AI model. Collecting and preparing high-quality data is crucial for training effective generative models (Provost and Fawcett 2013).

Data Collection

The first step in building a Generative AI model is to collect a dataset that is representative of the task at hand. This involves gathering data from various sources, such as:

Public Datasets: Many public datasets are available for different types of generative tasks, including image generation (e.g., CIFAR-10, ImageNet), text generation (e.g., Wikipedia, OpenAI's GPT-3 dataset), and music generation (e.g., MAESTRO).

Custom Data Collection: If public datasets do not meet your needs, you may need to collect your own data. This could involve web scraping, data mining, or manually curating datasets.

Data Preprocessing

Once you have collected the data, the next step is to preprocess it to ensure it is suitable for training. This involves several steps:

Cleaning: Remove any noise, errors, or irrelevant information from the dataset.

Normalization: Scale numerical data to a standard range, such as [0, 1], to ensure consistent input to the model (LeCun, Leon Bottou, et al. 1998).

Tokenization: For text data, break down the text into individual tokens (words or subwords) that can be processed by the model (I. Goodfellow, Y. Bengio, and Courville 2016).

Augmentation: Apply data augmentation techniques to increase the diversity and size of the dataset, such as flipping, rotating, or cropping images (Shorten and Khoshgoftaar 2019).

Choosing the Right Model

Selecting the appropriate model architecture is crucial for the success of your Generative AI project. Different types of generative models are suited to different tasks (I. Goodfellow, Y. Bengio, and Courville 2016).

Generative Adversarial Networks (GANs)

GANs are well-suited for tasks that involve generating high-quality images, videos, and other types of media. They consist of a generator and a discriminator that are trained simultaneously in a competitive setting (I. Goodfellow, Pouget-Abadie, et al. 2014).

Applications: Image generation, video generation, data augmentation, style transfer.

Python Example:

```python
import tensorflow as tf
from tensorflow.keras.layers import Dense, Reshape, Flatten,
    Conv2D, Conv2DTranspose, LeakyReLU
from tensorflow.keras.models import Sequential

# Generator model
def build_generator():
    model = Sequential()
    model.add(Dense(128 * 7 * 7, activation="relu", input_dim
        =100))
    model.add(Reshape((7, 7, 128)))
    model.add(Conv2DTranspose(128, kernel_size=4, strides=2,
        padding="same"))
    model.add(LeakyReLU(alpha=0.01))
    model.add(Conv2DTranspose(64, kernel_size=4, strides=2,
        padding="same"))
    model.add(LeakyReLU(alpha=0.01))
    model.add(Conv2D(1, kernel_size=7, activation="tanh",
        padding="same"))
    return model

# Discriminator model
def build_discriminator():
    model = Sequential()
    model.add(Conv2D(64, kernel_size=3, strides=2, input_shape
        =(28, 28, 1), padding="same"))
```

```python
    model.add(LeakyReLU(alpha=0.01))
    model.add(Conv2D(128, kernel_size=3, strides=2, padding="
        same"))
    model.add(LeakyReLU(alpha=0.01))
    model.add(Flatten())
    model.add(Dense(1, activation="sigmoid"))
    return model

# Compile and train the GAN
def compile_gan(generator, discriminator):
    discriminator.compile(loss="binary_crossentropy",
        optimizer="adam", metrics=["accuracy"])
    discriminator.trainable = False
    gan_input = tf.keras.Input(shape=(100,))
    gan_output = discriminator(generator(gan_input))
    gan = tf.keras.Model(gan_input, gan_output)
    gan.compile(loss="binary_crossentropy", optimizer="adam")
    return gan
```

Variational Autoencoders (VAEs)

VAEs are suitable for tasks that require learning a latent representation of the data. They can generate new data points by sampling from the learned latent space (Kingma and Welling 2013).

Applications: Image generation, anomaly detection, data compression, representation learning.

Python Example:

```python
import tensorflow as tf
from tensorflow.keras.layers import Input, Dense, Lambda,
    Layer, Add, Multiply
from tensorflow.keras.models import Model
from tensorflow.keras import backend as K

# VAE encoder model
def build_vae_encoder(input_shape, latent_dim):
    inputs = Input(shape=input_shape)
    x = Dense(128, activation="relu")(inputs)
    z_mean = Dense(latent_dim)(x)
```

```python
    z_log_var = Dense(latent_dim)(x)
    return Model(inputs, [z_mean, z_log_var])

# VAE sampling function
def sampling(args):
    z_mean, z_log_var = args
    epsilon = K.random_normal(shape=K.shape(z_mean), mean=0.,
        stddev=1.)
    return z_mean + K.exp(z_log_var) * epsilon

# VAE decoder model
def build_vae_decoder(latent_dim, output_shape):
    latent_inputs = Input(shape=(latent_dim,))
    x = Dense(128, activation="relu")(latent_inputs)
    outputs = Dense(output_shape, activation="sigmoid")(x)
    return Model(latent_inputs, outputs)

# VAE complete model
def build_vae(input_shape, latent_dim):
    encoder = build_vae_encoder(input_shape, latent_dim)
    decoder = build_vae_decoder(latent_dim, input_shape[0])
    inputs = Input(shape=input_shape)
    z_mean, z_log_var = encoder(inputs)
    z = Lambda(sampling)([z_mean, z_log_var])
    outputs = decoder(z)
    vae = Model(inputs, outputs)
    vae.add_loss(-0.5 * K.sum(1 + z_log_var - K.square(z_mean)
        - K.exp(z_log_var), axis=-1))
    vae.compile(optimizer="adam", loss="binary_crossentropy")
    return vae
```

Autoregressive Models

Autoregressive models are ideal for tasks that involve generating sequential data, such as text, music, and time series (Oord, Dieleman, et al. 2016).

Applications: Text generation, music composition, speech synthesis, time series forecasting.

Python Example:

```python
import tensorflow as tf
from tensorflow.keras.layers import Embedding, LSTM, Dense
from tensorflow.keras.models import Sequential

# Autoregressive model for text generation
def build_autoregressive_model(vocab_size, embedding_dim,
    lstm_units):
    model = Sequential()
    model.add(Embedding(vocab_size, embedding_dim))
    model.add(LSTM(lstm_units, return_sequences=True))
    model.add(LSTM(lstm_units))
    model.add(Dense(vocab_size, activation="softmax"))
    model.compile(optimizer="adam", loss="
        sparse_categorical_crossentropy")
    return model
```

Flow-based Models

Flow-based models are useful for tasks that require exact likelihood estimation and efficient sampling. They transform a simple base distribution into the target distribution using invertible transformations (Dinh, Sohl-Dickstein, and S. Bengio 2016).

Applications: Density estimation, image generation, latent variable modeling.

Python Example:

```python
import tensorflow as tf
from tensorflow.keras.layers import Input, Dense
from tensorflow.keras.models import Model

# Simple RealNVP flow-based model
class RealNVP(tf.keras.Model):
    def __init__(self, num_coupling_layers, input_shape):
        super(RealNVP, self).__init__()
        self.num_coupling_layers = num_coupling_layers
        self.input_shape = input_shape
        self.coupling_layers = [self.build_coupling_layer() for
            _ in range(num_coupling_layers)]
```

```python
def build_coupling_layer(self):
    input = Input(shape=self.input_shape)
    x = Dense(128, activation="relu")(input)
    x = Dense(128, activation="relu")(x)
    output = Dense(self.input_shape[0])(x)
    return Model(input, output)

def call(self, x, training=False):
    log_det_J = 0
    for coupling_layer in self.coupling_layers:
        x = x + coupling_layer(x)
        log_det_J += tf.reduce_sum(coupling_layer(x), axis
            =1)
    return x, log_det_J
```

Building and Training the Model

Once you have selected the appropriate model, the next step is to build and train it. This involves several key steps:

Model Architecture

Define the architecture of your generative model, including the number of layers, types of layers (e.g., convolutional, recurrent), and activation functions. Popular deep learning frameworks such as TensorFlow, PyTorch, and Keras provide tools for building and customizing model architectures (I. Goodfellow, Y. Bengio, and Courville 2016).

Loss Functions

Choose the appropriate loss function for training your generative model. The loss function measures the difference between the generated data and the real data, guiding the optimization process (I. Goodfellow, Pouget-Abadie, et al. 2014).

GANs: Use the adversarial loss function, which involves optimizing the generator and discriminator simultaneously.

VAEs: Use the evidence lower bound (ELBO) loss, which combines a reconstruction term and a regularization term (Kingma and Welling 2013).

Autoregressive Models: Use the maximum likelihood estimation (MLE) loss, which involves maximizing the probability of the observed data given the model (Oord, Dieleman, et al. 2016).

Flow-based Models: Use the change of variables formula to compute the likelihood of the data and optimize it directly (Dinh, Sohl-Dickstein, and S. Bengio 2016).

Training Process

Train your generative model using an optimization algorithm such as stochastic gradient descent (SGD) or Adam. This involves iterating through the training data, updating the model parameters to minimize the loss function (Kingma and Ba 2014).

Batch Size: Choose an appropriate batch size for training, balancing between computational efficiency and model performance.

Learning Rate: Set the learning rate for the optimizer, which determines the step size for parameter updates. Use learning rate schedules to adjust the learning rate during training.

Epochs: Train the model for a sufficient number of epochs to ensure convergence. Monitor the loss and performance metrics to avoid overfitting (I. Goodfellow, Y. Bengio, and Courville 2016).

Evaluating and Fine-Tuning the Model

After training the model, it is essential to evaluate its performance and fine-tune it to achieve the best results.

Evaluation Metrics

Use appropriate evaluation metrics to assess the quality of the generated data and the model's performance (Salimans et al. 2016).

GANs: Use metrics such as Inception Score (IS) and Frechet Inception Distance (FID) to evaluate the quality and diversity of generated images.

VAEs: Use metrics such as reconstruction error and log-likelihood to assess the model's ability to generate realistic data.

Autoregressive Models: Use metrics such as perplexity and BLEU score to evaluate the quality of generated text and sequences.

Hyperparameter Tuning

Fine-tune the hyperparameters of your model to improve its performance. This involves experimenting with different values for parameters such as learning rate, batch size, number of layers, and regularization techniques (Bergstra and Y. Bengio 2012).

Grid Search: Perform a grid search to systematically explore combinations of hyperparameters and identify the best configuration.

Random Search: Perform a random search to sample hyperparameter combinations randomly and efficiently.

Regularization Techniques

Apply regularization techniques to prevent overfitting and improve the generalization of your model (Srivastava et al. 2014).

Dropout: Randomly drop a fraction of neurons during training to force the model to learn redundant representations.

L2 Regularization: Add a penalty term to the loss function based on the sum of the squared weights to prevent large weight values.

Tools and Frameworks

Several tools and frameworks facilitate the development of Generative AI models, providing pre-built modules, high-level APIs, and optimization tools.

TensorFlow

TensorFlow is an open-source deep learning framework developed by Google. It supports a wide range of machine learning and deep learning applications, providing tools for building and training neural networks (Abadi et al. 2016).

TensorFlow Hub: A repository of pre-trained models and reusable components for building generative models.

TensorFlow Model Garden: A collection of state-of-the-art models and tools for training and evaluating generative models.

PyTorch

PyTorch is an open-source deep learning framework developed by Facebook. It is known for its dynamic computation graph and ease of use, making it popular in both research and industry (Paszke et al. 2019).

torchvision: A library that provides tools for image processing and pre-trained models for building generative models.

Hugging Face Transformers: A library that provides pre-trained transformer models and tools for natural language processing tasks (Wolf et al. 2020).

Keras

Keras is an open-source neural network library that runs on top of TensorFlow. It offers a user-friendly API for quickly prototyping and building deep learning models (Chollet et al. 2015).

Keras Applications: A collection of pre-trained models and tools for building and training generative models.

From Idea to Implementation

Building your own Generative AI models involves a series of steps, from data collection and preparation to model selection, training, and evaluation. By following these steps and leveraging the tools and frameworks available, you can create powerful generative models that push the boundaries of what AI can achieve. Whether you are generating realistic images, composing music, or creating personalized content, the journey from idea to implementation is both challenging and rewarding. Embrace the process, experiment with different approaches, and continue to explore the exciting world of Generative AI (I. Goodfellow, Y. Bengio, and Courville 2016).

Chapter 10

The Ethical AI Movement and Your Role

Joining the Ethical AI Movement

As Generative AI continues to advance, the importance of ethical considerations and responsible practices becomes ever more critical. The Ethical AI Movement seeks to ensure that AI technologies are developed and deployed in ways that are fair, transparent, and beneficial to all. This chapter explores the core principles of ethical AI, the role of various stakeholders, and how you can contribute to the movement (B. D. Mittelstadt et al. 2016).

Core Principles of Ethical AI

Ethical AI encompasses several key principles that guide the development and deployment of AI technologies:

Fairness

Fairness in AI involves ensuring that AI systems do not perpetuate or amplify biases, and that they treat all individuals and groups equitably

(Barocas, Hardt, and Narayanan 2017).

Equitable Access: AI technologies should be accessible to all individuals, regardless of their socioeconomic status, geographic location, or other factors (Whittaker et al. 2018).

Bias Mitigation: Developers must actively work to identify and mitigate biases in AI models and datasets (Mehrabi et al. 2021).

Transparency

Transparency involves making the operations and decision-making processes of AI systems understandable and accessible to users and stakeholders (Lipton 2018).

Explainability: AI systems should provide clear explanations for their decisions and actions (Gilpin et al. 2018).

Open Communication: Organizations should be open about how AI systems are developed, deployed, and used (Weller 2019).

Accountability

Accountability ensures that developers, organizations, and users are responsible for the ethical implications of AI systems (Diakopoulos 2016).

Responsibility: Developers and organizations must take responsibility for the impact of their AI systems.

Regulation and Oversight: Effective regulatory frameworks and oversight mechanisms should be in place to ensure accountability (Wachter and B. Mittelstadt 2019).

Privacy

Privacy involves protecting individuals' personal data and ensuring that AI systems comply with data protection regulations (Davidson, De Filippi, and Potts 2017).

Data Protection: AI systems must adhere to data protection laws and regulations, such as GDPR (Voigt and Von dem Bussche 2017).

Consent: Individuals should have control over how their data is used and should provide informed consent for its use in AI systems (Floridi et al. 2018).

The Role of Various Stakeholders

Ensuring ethical AI requires the collaboration and commitment of various stakeholders, including developers, organizations, policymakers, and the public.

Developers and Researchers

Developers and researchers play a crucial role in designing and building ethical AI systems.

Ethical Design: Integrate ethical considerations into the design and development of AI systems from the outset (B. D. Mittelstadt et al. 2016).

Continuous Learning: Stay informed about the latest developments in AI ethics and actively seek to improve ethical practices.

Organizations

Organizations that deploy AI systems must prioritize ethical considerations in their operations.

Ethical Guidelines: Establish and adhere to ethical guidelines for the development and deployment of AI systems (Jobin, Ienca, and Vayena 2019).

Training and Education: Provide training and education on AI ethics to employees and stakeholders.

Policymakers

Policymakers play a critical role in creating regulatory frameworks that ensure the ethical use of AI (Wachter and B. Mittelstadt 2019).

Regulation: Develop and enforce regulations that promote ethical AI practices.

Public Engagement: Engage with the public to understand their concerns and perspectives on AI ethics.

The Public

The public has a vital role in advocating for ethical AI and holding organizations and policymakers accountable.

Awareness and Advocacy: Stay informed about AI ethics and advocate for ethical practices and policies.

Participation: Participate in public discussions and decision-making processes related to AI ethics.

How You Can Contribute to Ethical AI

Whether you are a developer, researcher, or concerned citizen, there are several ways you can contribute to the Ethical AI Movement.

Education and Awareness

Educate yourself and others about the ethical implications of AI and the importance of ethical practices (Floridi et al. 2018).

Reading and Research: Stay informed about the latest developments in AI ethics by reading articles, books, and research papers.

Workshops and Seminars: Attend workshops, seminars, and conferences on AI ethics to deepen your understanding and connect with others in the field.

Advocacy and Engagement

Advocate for ethical AI practices and engage with organizations, policymakers, and the public to promote ethical considerations.

Public Speaking: Share your knowledge and perspectives on AI ethics through public speaking engagements, such as talks, panels, and webinars.

Writing and Publishing: Write articles, blog posts, and opinion pieces on AI ethics to raise awareness and encourage discussion.

Ethical Development Practices

If you are involved in developing AI systems, integrate ethical considerations into your development practices (B. D. Mittelstadt et al. 2016).

Bias Audits: Regularly audit your AI models and datasets for biases and take corrective actions as needed (Barocas, Hardt, and Narayanan 2017).

User-Centric Design: Design AI systems with the needs and perspectives of users in mind, ensuring that they are fair, transparent, and accountable (Diakopoulos 2016).

Collaboration and Community Building

Collaborate with others in the AI ethics community to share knowledge, resources, and best practices (Jobin, Ienca, and Vayena 2019).

Networking: Connect with other professionals and organizations working on AI ethics through networking events, forums, and social media.

Community Initiatives: Participate in or lead community initiatives that promote ethical AI, such as hackathons, study groups, and advocacy campaigns.

Your Role in Shaping the Future of AI

The Ethical AI Movement is a collective effort that requires the participation and commitment of individuals, organizations, and society as a whole. By understanding the core principles of ethical AI, recognizing the roles of various stakeholders, and actively contributing to the movement, you can help shape a future where AI technologies are developed and deployed in ways that are fair, transparent, and beneficial to all. Together, we can ensure that AI serves as a force for good, enhancing human capabilities and promoting a just and equitable society (Floridi et al. 2018).

Epilogue

The Dawn of a New Era

As we stand on the brink of a new era defined by the incredible potential of Generative AI, we are reminded of the profound impact that technology can have on our lives. This book has journeyed through the foundational concepts of Generative AI, its diverse applications, and the ethical considerations that must guide its development and deployment. As we conclude, it is essential to reflect on the responsibilities we hold and the future we envision.

Harnessing Creativity and Innovation

Generative AI has opened up new frontiers in creativity and innovation, allowing us to explore possibilities that were once beyond our reach. From creating art and music to advancing healthcare and education, the applications of Generative AI are as boundless as human imagination. It empowers us to push the boundaries of what is possible, transforming the way we live, work, and interact with the world (Elgammal et al. 2017).

Yet, as we harness this power, we must remember that technology is a tool, and its true value lies in how we choose to use it. The creations of Generative AI reflect our aspirations, values, and vision for the future. It is up to us to ensure that these creations serve to enrich lives, foster inclusivity, and promote the well-being of all (Briot, Hadjeres, and Pachet 2020).

The Ethical Imperative

The ethical implications of Generative AI are profound, and they call for a collective commitment to fairness, transparency, accountability, and privacy. As we have explored, addressing bias, ensuring fairness, and protecting privacy are not just technical challenges but moral imperatives. They require continuous vigilance, reflection, and action from all of us—developers, researchers, policymakers, organizations, and citizens (Floridi et al. 2018).

The ethical AI movement is more than a set of guidelines; it is a call to action to build a future where AI technologies enhance human dignity and respect fundamental rights. By fostering a culture of ethical awareness and promoting responsible practices, we can ensure that Generative AI contributes positively to society (B. D. Mittelstadt et al. 2016).

A Vision for the Future

As we look to the future, we envision a world where Generative AI is seamlessly integrated into our daily lives, augmenting our capabilities and opening up new possibilities. It is a world where AI acts as a creative partner, enhancing human potential and enabling us to tackle complex challenges with innovative solutions.

In this future, AI is not a distant, opaque entity but a transparent, understandable, and trustworthy companion. It is a technology that respects our privacy, upholds our values, and works in harmony with our goals. It is a future where AI technologies are accessible to all, bridging divides and fostering a more inclusive and equitable society (Floridi et al. 2018).

Your Role in Shaping the Future

The journey of Generative AI is just beginning, and each of us has a role to play in shaping its trajectory. Whether you are an AI developer pushing the boundaries of what is possible, a policymaker crafting regulations that protect and empower, an educator inspiring the next generation of AI leaders, or a concerned citizen advocating for ethical practices, your contribution matters (Floridi et al. 2018).

By embracing our roles and responsibilities, we can collectively steer the development of Generative AI towards a future that is innovative, ethical, and inclusive. Let us remain curious, vigilant, and committed to the principles that ensure AI serves the greater good (Barocas, Hardt, and Narayanan 2017).

A Closing Thought

As we close this book, let us carry forward the insights, knowledge, and inspiration we have gained. Generative AI is not just a technological marvel; it is a testament to human ingenuity and our enduring quest for progress. It holds the promise of a brighter future, but it is up to us to realize that promise with wisdom, care, and a steadfast commitment to ethical principles (Floridi et al. 2018).

The dawn of a new era is upon us. Let us step into it with hope, determination, and a shared vision for a world where technology enhances our humanity and paves the way for a future of endless possibilities.

Thank you for joining us on this journey. Together, we can shape the future of Generative AI and create a legacy that will inspire generations to come.

Bibliography

Abadi, Martín et al. (2016). "TensorFlow: A System for Large-Scale Machine Learning". In: *12th USENIX Symposium on Operating Systems Design and Implementation (OSDI 16)*, pp. 265–283.

Aggarwal, Charu C. and Tarek Abdelzaher (2018). "Towards Anonymizing User Data in Social Networks". In: *Communications of the ACM* 55.12, pp. 24–26.

Agrawal, Rakesh, Tomasz Imielinski, and Arun Swami (1993). "Mining Association Rules between Sets of Items in Large Databases". In: *ACM SIGMOD Record*. Vol. 22. 2. ACM, pp. 207–216.

AI, Squirrel (2019). *Empowering Futures Through AI-Driven Personalized Learning*. URL: https://www.squirrelai.com/.

Alarcon, Nefi (2018). "AI Can Generate Synthetic MRIs to Advance Medical Research". In: *NVIDIA Developer Blog*. URL: https://developer.nvidia.com/blog/ai-can-generate-synthetic-mris-to-advance-medical-research/.

Alpaydin, Ethem (2020). *Introduction to Machine Learning*. MIT Press.

An, Jinwon and Sungzoon Cho (2015). "Variational Autoencoder based Anomaly Detection using Reconstruction Probability". In: *SNU Data Mining Center* 110.7, pp. 1–18.

Antoniou, Antreas, Amos Storkey, and Harrison Edwards (2017). "Data Augmentation Generative Adversarial Networks". In: *arXiv preprint arXiv:1711.04340*.

Arjovsky, Martin, Soumith Chintala, and Léon Bottou (2017). "Wasserstein GAN". In: *arXiv preprint arXiv:1701.07875*.

Autodesk (2019). *Generative Design for Manufacturing | Autodesk Fusion*. URL: https://www.autodesk.com/generative-design/.

Barocas, Solon, Moritz Hardt, and Arvind Narayanan (2017). *Fairness in Machine Learning*. Nips tutorial.

— (2019). "Fairness and Machine Learning". In: *Nips tutorial* 1.2, pp. 1–45.

Baum, Zachary and David B. Agus (2020). "Artificial Intelligence in Medical Imaging: Opportunities, Applications and Risks". In: *Nature Reviews*.

Bengio, Yoshua (2009). "Learning Deep Architectures for AI". In: *Foundations and Trends® in Machine Learning* 2.1, pp. 1–127.

Bengio, Yoshua, Aaron Courville, and Pascal Vincent (2013). "Representation Learning: A Review and New Perspectives". In: *IEEE Transactions on Pattern Analysis and Machine Intelligence* 35.8, pp. 1798–1828.

Bergstra, James and Yoshua Bengio (2012). "Random Search for Hyper-Parameter Optimization". In: *Journal of Machine Learning Research*. Vol. 13. 2, pp. 281–305.

Binns, Reuben (2018). "Fairness in Machine Learning: Lessons from Political Philosophy". In: *Proceedings of the 2018 Conference on Fairness, Accountability, and Transparency*, pp. 149–159.

Bishop, Christopher M (2006). *Pattern Recognition and Machine Learning*. Springer.

Booth, Andy (2019). "AI-Driven NPCs in Red Dead Redemption 2". In: *Game Developer Conference*.

Box, George EP et al. (2015). *Time Series Analysis: Forecasting and Control*. John Wiley & Sons.

Breiman, Leo (2001). "Random Forests". In: *Machine Learning* 45.1, pp. 5–32.

Breiman, Leo et al. (1984). *Classification and Regression Trees*. CRC press.

Briot, Jean-Pierre, Gaetan Hadjeres, and Francois-David Pachet (2020). *Deep Learning Techniques for Music Generation: A Survey*. Springer.

Brynjolfsson, Erik, Daniel Rock, and Chad Syverson (2017). "Artificial Intelligence and the Modern Productivity Paradox: A Clash of Expectations and Statistics". In: *National Bureau of Economic Research* 23767.

Buolamwini, Joy and Timnit Gebru (2018). "Gender Shades: Intersectional Accuracy Disparities in Commercial Gender Classification". In: *Proceedings of the 1st Conference on Fairness, Accountability and Transparency*, pp. 77–91.

Calo, Ryan (2017). "Artificial Intelligence Policy: A Primer and Roadmap". In: *UC Davis Law Review* 51, p. 399.

Chen, Ting et al. (2020). "A Simple Framework for Contrastive Learning of Visual Representations". In: *arXiv preprint arXiv:2002.05709*.

Chesney, Robert and Danielle Citron (2019). "Deep Fakes: A Looming Challenge for Privacy, Democracy, and National Security". In: *California Law Review* 107, pp. 1753–1820.

Cho, Kyunghyun et al. (2014). "Learning Phrase Representations using RNN Encoder-Decoder for Statistical Machine Translation". In: *arXiv preprint arXiv:1406.1078*.

Chollet, François et al. (2015). "Keras". In: *GitHub. Note: https://github. com/fchollet/keras*. Vol. 2015.

Christie's (2018). "Is Artificial Intelligence Set to Become Art's Next Medium?" In: *Christie's*. URL: `https : / / www . christies . com / features / A - collaboration - between - two - artists - one - human-one-a-machine-9332-1.aspx`.

Commission, European (2019). *Ethics Guidelines for Trustworthy AI*. European Union.

Cortes, Corinna and Vladimir Vapnik (1995). "Support-Vector Networks". In: *Machine Learning* 20.3, pp. 273–297.

Cover, Thomas and Peter Hart (1967). "Nearest Neighbor Pattern Classification". In: *IEEE Transactions on Information Theory* 13.1, pp. 21–27.

Covington, Paul, Jay Adams, and Emre Sargin (2016). "Deep Neural Networks for YouTube Recommendations". In: *Proceedings of the 10th ACM Conference on Recommender Systems*, pp. 191–198.

Crockett, Shomari (2023). "AI-Driven Virtual Reality: Creating Dynamic and Interactive Virtual Environments". In: *Medium*. URL: `https : / / medium . com / @shomariccrockett / ai - driven - virtual - reality - creating - dynamic - and - interactive - virtual-environments-6137fbfd2d2d`.

Danks, David and Alex John London (2017). "Algorithmic Bias in Autonomous Systems". In: *Proceedings of the 26th International Joint Conference on Artificial Intelligence*, pp. 4691–4697.

Davidson, Sinclair, Primavera De Filippi, and Jason Potts (2017). "Distributed Ledger Technologies for Decentralized Optimization". In: *Proceedings of the 1st Workshop on Cryptocurrencies and Blockchains for Distributed Systems*, pp. 1–6.

Dean, Jeff et al. (2012). "Large Scale Distributed Deep Networks". In: *Advances in Neural Information Processing Systems*. Vol. 25.

Devlin, Jacob et al. (2018). "BERT: Pre-Training of Deep Bidirectional Transformers for Language Understanding". In: *arXiv preprint arXiv:1810.04805*.

Dhariwal, Prafulla et al. (2020). "Jukebox: A Generative Model for Music". In.

Diakopoulos, Nicholas (2016). "Accountability in Algorithmic Decision Making". In: *Communications of the ACM*. Vol. 59. 2. ACM, pp. 56–62.

Dinh, Laurent, Jascha Sohl-Dickstein, and Samy Bengio (2016). "Density Estimation using Real NVP". In: *International Conference on Learning Representations (ICLR)*.

Doersch, Carl, Abhinav Gupta, and Alexei A Efros (2015). "Unsupervised Learning of Visual Representations by Solving Jigsaw Puzzles". In: *arXiv preprint arXiv:1506.06972*.

Domingos, Pedro (2012). "A Few Useful Things to Know about Machine Learning". In: *Communications of the ACM* 55.10, pp. 78–87.

Doshi-Velez, Finale and Been Kim (2017). "Towards a Rigorous Science of Interpretable Machine Learning". In: *arXiv preprint arXiv:1702.08608*.

Dosovitskiy, Alexey et al. (2020). "An Image is Worth 16x16 Words: Transformers for Image Recognition at Scale". In: *arXiv preprint arXiv:2010.11929*.

Duolingo (2023). "Introducing Duolingo Max: The Future of Language Learning with AI". In: *Duolingo Blog*. URL: `https://blog.duolingo.com/duolingo-max/`.

El Emam, Khaled, Luis Mosquera, and Juan Carlos Hu (2021). "Anonymizing Data for Generative AI: A Case Study". In: *IEEE Access* 9, pp. 32736–32747.

Elgammal, Ahmed et al. (2017). "Can: Creative Adversarial Networks, Generating "Art" by Learning About Styles and Deviating from Style Norms". In: *arXiv preprint arXiv:1706.07068*.

Feigenbaum, Edward A. and Avron Barr (1983). *The Handbook of Artificial Intelligence, Volume 1*. William Kaufmann.

Floridi, Luciano et al. (2018). "AI4People—An Ethical Framework for a Good AI Society: Opportunities, Risks, Principles, and Recommendations". In: *Minds and Machines* 28.4, pp. 689–707.

Frid-Adar, Maayan et al. (2018). "GAN-Based Medical Image Augmentation for Increased CNN Performance in Brain Tumor Classification". In: *arXiv preprint arXiv:1803.01229*.

Friedman, Jerome, Trevor Hastie, and Robert Tibshirani (2001). *The Elements of Statistical Learning*. Springer.

Games, Hello (n.d.). "No Man's Sky: Procedural Content Generation in Gaming". In: *No Man's Sky* (). URL: `https://www.nomanssky.com/`.

Games, Rockstar (n.d.). "Red Dead Redemption 2: AI in Gaming". In: *Rockstar Games* (). URL: `https://www.rockstargames.com/reddeadredemption2/`.

Geman, Stuart, Elisa Bienenstock, and Rene Doursat (1992). "Neural Networks and the Bias/Variance Dilemma". In: *Neural Computation* 4.1, pp. 1–58.

Geron, Aurelien (2019). *Hands-On Machine Learning with Scikit-Learn, Keras, and TensorFlow: Concepts, Tools, and Techniques to Build Intelligent Systems*. O'Reilly Media.

Gilpin, Leilani H et al. (2018). "Explaining Explanations: An Overview of Interpretability of Machine Learning". In: *arXiv preprint arXiv:1806.00069*.

Goodfellow, Ian, Yoshua Bengio, and Aaron Courville (2016). *Deep Learning*. MIT press.

Goodfellow, Ian, Jean Pouget-Abadie, et al. (2014). "Generative Adversarial Nets". In: *Advances in neural information processing systems* 27.

Goodfellow, Ian J, Jonathon Shlens, and Christian Szegedy (2014). "Explaining and Harnessing Adversarial Examples". In: *arXiv preprint arXiv:1412.6572*.

Google and Zalando (2016). "Project Muze: Fashion inspired by you, designed by code". In: *Google Blog*. URL: `https://blog.google/`

`around-the-globe/google-europe/project-muze-fashion-inspired-by-you/`.

Graves, Alex, Abdel-rahman Mohamed, and Geoffrey Hinton (2013). "Speech Recognition with Deep Recurrent Neural Networks". In: *IEEE International Conference on Acoustics, Speech and Signal Processing (ICASSP)*, pp. 6645–6649.

Grover, Aditya, Manoj Dhar, and Stefano Ermon (2018). "Flow-GAN: Combining Maximum Likelihood and Adversarial Learning in Generative Models". In: *arXiv preprint arXiv:1803.04468*.

Hardt, Moritz, Eric Price, and Nathan Srebro (2016). "Equality of Opportunity in Supervised Learning". In: *Advances in Neural Information Processing Systems* 29, pp. 3315–3323.

Hastie, Trevor, Robert Tibshirani, and Jerome Friedman (2009a). *The Elements of Statistical Learning: Data Mining, Inference, and Prediction*. Springer Science & Business Media.

— (2009b). *Unsupervised Learning: The Estimation of Principal Components*. Springer.

Haykin, Simon (1994). *Neural Networks: A Comprehensive Foundation*. Prentice Hall.

He, Kaiming et al. (2016). "Deep Residual Learning for Image Recognition". In: *Proceedings of the IEEE Conference on Computer Vision and Pattern Recognition*, pp. 770–778.

Heaton, James B, Nicholas G Polson, and Jan Hendrik Witte (2017). "Deep Learning for Finance: Predicting the Market with AI". In: *arXiv preprint arXiv:1703.04976*.

Hochreiter, Sepp and Jürgen Schmidhuber (1997). "Long Short-Term Memory". In: *Neural Computation* 9.8, pp. 1735–1780.

Holmes, Wayne, Maya Bialik, and Charles Fadel (2019). "Artificial Intelligence in Education". In: *Center for Curriculum Redesign*.

Holstein, Kenneth et al. (2019). "Improving Fairness in Machine Learning Systems: What Do Industry Practitioners Need?" In: *Proceedings of the 2019 CHI Conference on Human Factors in Computing Systems*, pp. 1–16.

Hosmer, David W, Stanley Lemeshow, and Rodney X Sturdivant (2013). *Applied Logistic Regression*. John Wiley & Sons.

IEEE (2019). "Ethically Aligned Design: A Vision for Prioritizing Human Well-being with Autonomous and Intelligent Systems". In:

The IEEE Global Initiative on Ethics of Autonomous and Intelligent Systems 3, pp. 1–62.

Isola, Phillip et al. (2017). "Image-to-Image Translation with Conditional Adversarial Networks". In: *Proceedings of the IEEE Conference on Computer Vision and Pattern Recognition*, pp. 1125–1134.

Jain, Anil K, M Narasimha Murty, and Patrick J Flynn (1999). "Data Clustering: A Review". In: *ACM computing surveys (CSUR)* 31.3, pp. 264–323.

Jain, Shweta and Nikita Thakur (2019). "A Survey on Privacy-preserving Techniques for Model Training and Inference in Machine Learning". In: *Journal of Information Security and Applications* 48, p. 102392.

Jobin, Anna, Marcello Ienca, and Effy Vayena (2019). "The Global Landscape of AI Ethics Guidelines". In: *Nature Machine Intelligence* 1.9, pp. 389–399.

Jolliffe, Ian (2011). *Principal Component Analysis*. Springer.

Kamiran, Faisal and Toon Calders (2012). "Data Preprocessing Techniques for Classification without Discrimination". In: *Knowledge and Information Systems* 33.1, pp. 1–33.

Kandel, Eric R, James H Schwartz, and Thomas M Jessell (2000). *Principles of Neural Science*. McGraw-Hill.

Karras, Tero, Samuli Laine, and Timo Aila (2019). "A Style-Based Generator Architecture for Generative Adversarial Networks". In: *Proceedings of the IEEE/CVF Conference on Computer Vision and Pattern Recognition*, pp. 4401–4410.

Kaul, Ashok et al. (2020). "AI-based Drug Discovery and Development". In: *Journal of Drug Discovery* 15.

Kingma, Diederik P and Jimmy Ba (2014). "Adam: A Method for Stochastic Optimization". In: *arXiv preprint arXiv:1412.6980*.

Kingma, Diederik P and Prafulla Dhariwal (2018). "Glow: Generative Flow with Invertible 1x1 Convolutions". In: *Advances in Neural Information Processing Systems*. Vol. 31, pp. 10215–10224.

Kingma, Diederik P and Max Welling (2013). "Auto-Encoding Variational Bayes". In: *arXiv preprint arXiv:1312.6114*.

— (2019). "An Introduction to Variational Autoencoders". In: *Foundations and Trends® in Machine Learning* 12.4, pp. 307–392.

Konda, Vijay R and John N Tsitsiklis (2000). "Actor-Critic Algorithms".
   In: *Advances in Neural Information Processing Systems*, pp. 1008–
   1014.
Kotsiantis, Sotiris, Dimitris Kanellopoulos, and Panayiotis Pintelas
   (2006). "Data Preprocessing for Supervised Learning". In: *Interna-*
   tional Journal of Computer Science 1.2, pp. 111–117.
Krizhevsky, Alex, Ilya Sutskever, and Geoffrey E. Hinton (2012). "ImageNet Classification with Deep Convolutional Neural Networks".
   In: *Advances in Neural Information Processing Systems*. Vol. 25,
   pp. 1097–1105.
Larsen, Anders Boesen Lindbo et al. (2015). "Autoencoding beyond Pixels using a Learned Similarity Metric". In: *arXiv preprint*
   arXiv:1512.09300.
LeCun, Yann, Yoshua Bengio, and Geoffrey Hinton (2015). "Deep
   Learning". In: *Nature* 521.7553, pp. 436–444.
LeCun, Yann, Bernhard Boser, et al. (1989). "Backpropagation Applied
   to Handwritten Zip Code Recognition". In: *Neural Computation* 1.4,
   pp. 541–551.
LeCun, Yann, Leon Bottou, et al. (1998). "Gradient-Based Learning Ap-
   plied to Document Recognition". In: *Proceedings of the IEEE*. Vol. 86.
   11, pp. 2278–2324.
LeCun, Yann, Fu Jie Huang, and Léon Bottou (2006). "A Tutorial on
   Energy-Based Learning". In: *Predicting Structured Data* 1.0, pp. 1–
   59.
Li, Xinyang et al. (2019). "Deep Learning for Financial Risk Management". In: *Journal of Risk and Financial Management* 12.2, p. 55.
Lipton, Zachary C (2018). "The Mythos of Model Interpretability". In:
   Queue 16.3, pp. 31–57.
Liu, Pengfei, Zhengwei Gao, and Guangning Huang (2019). "Gen-
   erative Model Based on the Conditional Variational Autoen-
   coder for Controllable Sentence Generation". In: *arXiv preprint*
   arXiv:1907.02431.
Liu, Xuan, Wei Zhang, Chao Zhang, et al. (2019). "Chinese Language
   Learning with AI". In: *Journal of Educational Technology*.
Lloyd, Stuart (1982). "Least Squares Quantization in PCM". In: *IEEE*
   Transactions on Information Theory 28.2, pp. 129–137.

Maaten, Laurens van der and Geoffrey Hinton (2008). "Visualizing Data using t-SNE". In: *Journal of Machine Learning Research* 9.11, pp. 2579–2605.

McCarthy, John et al. (2006). "The Dartmouth Conference". In: *AI Magazine* 27.4, pp. 12–14.

Medicine, Insilico (2023). "Insilico Medicine Successfully Discovered Potent, Selective, and Orally Bioavailable Small Molecule Inhibitor of CDK8 Using Generative AI". In: *Yahoo Finance*. URL: https : / / finance . yahoo . com / news / insilico - medicine - successfully-discovered-potent-130000507.html.

Mehrabi, Ninareh et al. (2021). "A Survey on Bias and Fairness in Machine Learning". In: *ACM Computing Surveys (CSUR)* 54.6, pp. 1–35.

Milgram, Paul and Fumio Kishino (1994). "A Taxonomy of Mixed Reality Visual Displays". In: *IEICE Transactions on Information and Systems* 77.12, pp. 1321–1329.

Miotto, Riccardo et al. (2017). "Deep Patient: An Unsupervised Representation to Predict the Future of Patients from the Electronic Health Records". In: *Scientific Reports* 6, p. 26094.

Mitchell, Tom M (1997). *Machine Learning*. McGraw Hill.

Mittelstadt, Brent Daniel et al. (2016). "The Ethics of Algorithms: Mapping the Debate". In: *Big Data & Society* 3.2, pp. 1–21.

Mnih, Volodymyr et al. (2015). "Human-Level Control through Deep Reinforcement Learning". In: *Nature* 518.7540, pp. 529–533.

Mohri, Mehryar, Afshin Rostamizadeh, and Ameet Talwalkar (2018). *Foundations of Machine Learning*. MIT press.

Montgomery, Douglas C, Elizabeth A Peck, and G Geoffrey Vining (2012). *Introduction to Linear Regression Analysis*. John Wiley & Sons.

Mukherjee, Amartya, Arindam Banerjee, and Udita Garg (2020). "Designing with AI: AI-Powered Fashion and Apparel Generation". In: *Proceedings of the 11th International Conference on Artificial Intelligence in Fashion*.

Murphy, Kevin P (2012). *Machine Learning: A Probabilistic Perspective*. MIT press.

Murtagh, Fionn and Pierre Legendre (2014). "Ward's Hierarchical Clustering Method: Clustering Criterion and Agglomerative Algorithm". In: *Journal of Classification* 31.3, pp. 274–295.

Nair, Vinod and Geoffrey E Hinton (2010). "Rectified Linear Units Improve Restricted Boltzmann Machines". In: *Proceedings of the 27th International Conference on Machine Learning (ICML-10)*, pp. 807–814.

Nature (2024). "AI assistance for planning cancer treatment". In: *Nature*. URL: https://www.nature.com/articles/d41586-024-01431-8.

Olteanu, Alexandra et al. (2019). "Social Data: Biases, Methodological Pitfalls, and Ethical Boundaries". In: *Frontiers in Big Data* 2, p. 13.

Oord, Aaron van den, Sander Dieleman, et al. (2016). "WaveNet: A Generative Model for Raw Audio". In: *arXiv preprint arXiv:1609.03499*.

Oord, Aaron van den, Nal Kalchbrenner, and Koray Kavukcuoglu (2016). "Pixel Recurrent Neural Networks". In: *Proceedings of the 33rd International Conference on Machine Learning*. Vol. 48, pp. 1747–1756.

Paszke, Adam et al. (2019). "PyTorch: An Imperative Style, High-Performance Deep Learning Library". In: *Advances in Neural Information Processing Systems* 32.

Pearson, Karl (1901). "LIII. On Lines and Planes of Closest Fit to Systems of Points in Space". In: *The London, Edinburgh, and Dublin Philosophical Magazine and Journal of Science* 2.11, pp. 559–572.

Persado (2020). *Persado AI: Leading Generative AI Text Content Generation for Marketing*. URL: https://www.persado.com/.

Pleiss, Geoff et al. (2017). "On Fairness and Calibration". In: *Advances in Neural Information Processing Systems* 30, pp. 5680–5689.

Provost, Foster and Tom Fawcett (2013). *Data Science for Business: What You Need to Know about Data Mining and Data-Analytic Thinking*. O'Reilly Media, Inc.

Quinlan, J. Ross (1986). "Induction of Decision Trees". In: *Machine Learning* 1, pp. 81–106.

Radford, Alec, Luke Metz, and Soumith Chintala (2015). "Unsupervised Representation Learning with Deep Convolutional Generative Adversarial Networks". In: *International Conference on Learning Representations (ICLR)*.

Radford, Alec, Jeffrey Wu, et al. (2019). "Language Models are Unsupervised Multitask Learners". In: *OpenAI blog* 1.8, p. 9.

Raji, Inioluwa Deborah and Joy Buolamwini (2020). "Saving Face: Investigating the Ethical Concerns of Facial Recognition Auditing". In: *Proceedings of the AAAI/ACM Conference on AI, Ethics, and Society*, pp. 145–151.

Rezende, Danilo Jimenez and Shakir Mohamed (2015). "Variational Inference with Normalizing Flows". In: *International Conference on Machine Learning*, pp. 1530–1538.

Rosenblatt, Frank (1958). "The Perceptron: A Probabilistic Model for Information Storage and Organization in the Brain". In: *Psychological Review* 65.6, pp. 386–408.

Rössler, Andreas et al. (2019). "FaceForensics++: Learning to Detect Manipulated Facial Images". In: *Proceedings of the IEEE/CVF International Conference on Computer Vision*, pp. 1–11.

Rudin, Cynthia (2019). "Stop Explaining Black Box Machine Learning Models for High Stakes Decisions and Use Interpretable Models Instead". In: *Nature Machine Intelligence* 1.5, pp. 206–215.

Rumelhart, David E., Geoffrey E. Hinton, and Ronald J. Williams (1986). *Learning Representations by Back-Propagating Errors*. Nature.

Salesforce (2023). "Salesforce Announces Einstein GPT, the World's First Generative AI for CRM". In: *Salesforce News*. URL: `https://www.salesforce.com/news/press-releases/2023/03/07/einstein-generative-ai/`.

Salimans, Tim et al. (2016). "Improved Techniques for Training GANs". In: *Advances in Neural Information Processing Systems* 29, pp. 2234–2242.

School, Harvard Business (2018). "JP Morgan COIN: A Bank's Side Project Spells Disruption for the Legal Industry". In: *Digital Initiative*. URL: `https://d3.harvard.edu/platform-rctom/submission/jp-morgan-coin-a-banks-side-project-spells-disruption-for-the-legal-industry/`.

Sciforce (2023). "AI Revolution in EdTech: AI in Education Trends and Successful Cases". In: *Medium*. URL: `https://medium.com/sciforce/ai-revolution-in-edtech-ai-in-education-trends-and-successful-cases-7d5b7d69b77b`.

Seber, George AF and Alan J Lee (2012). *Linear Regression Analysis*. John Wiley & Sons.

Segler, Marwin H.S., Mike Preuss, and Mark P. Waller (2018). "Planning Chemical Syntheses with Deep Neural Networks and Symbolic AI". In: *Nature* 555, pp. 604–610.

Shaker, Noor, Julian Togelius, and Mark J Nelson (2016). *Procedural Content Generation in Games*. Springer.

Shorten, Connor and Taghi M Khoshgoftaar (2019). "A Survey on Image Data Augmentation for Deep Learning". In: *Journal of Big Data* 6.1, pp. 1–48.

Srivastava, Nitish et al. (2014). "Dropout: A Simple Way to Prevent Neural Networks from Overfitting". In: *Journal of Machine Learning Research* 15.1, pp. 1929–1958.

Sutskever, Ilya, Oriol Vinyals, and Quoc V. Le (2014). "Sequence to Sequence Learning with Neural Networks". In: *Advances in Neural Information Processing Systems*. Vol. 27, pp. 3104–3112.

Sutton, Richard S and Andrew G Barto (2018). *Reinforcement Learning: An Introduction*. MIT press.

Tian, Yujia, Takuya Kaneko, and Tetsuya Ogata (2014). "Learning from Between-class Examples for Deep Sound Recognition". In: *Proceedings of the 22nd ACM International Conference on Multimedia*, pp. 1185–1188.

Tomar, Navneet (2019). "AI in Education: Automating Content Creation". In: *Educational Technology*.

Topol, Eric (2019). *High-Performance Medicine: The Convergence of Human and Artificial Intelligence*. Nature.

Vaswani, Ashish et al. (2017). "Attention is All You Need". In: *Advances in Neural Information Processing Systems*. Vol. 30.

Verma, Sahil and Julia Rubin (2018). "Fairness Definitions Explained". In: *Proceedings of the 2018 Conference on Fairness, Accountability, and Transparency*, pp. 1–24.

Voigt, Paul and Axel Von dem Bussche (2017). *The EU General Data Protection Regulation (GDPR)*. Springer.

Vondrick, Carl, Hamed Pirsiavash, and Antonio Torralba (2016). "Generating Videos with Scene Dynamics". In: *Advances in Neural Information Processing Systems*. Vol. 29, pp. 613–621.

Wachter, Sandra and Brent Mittelstadt (2019). "Ethical and Social Implications of Algorithmic Decision Making". In: *The Oxford Handbook of Ethics of AI*.

Wang, Yaqing et al. (2020). "Generalizing from a Few Examples: A Survey on Few-Shot Learning". In: *ACM Computing Surveys (CSUR)* 53.3, pp. 1–34.

Watkins, Christopher JCH and Peter Dayan (1992). "Q-Learning". In: *Machine Learning* 8.3, pp. 279–292.

Weller, Adrian (2019). "Transparency: Motivations and Challenges". In: *Explainable AI: Interpreting, Explaining and Visualizing Deep Learning*. Springer, pp. 23–40.

Whittaker, Meredith et al. (2018). *AI Now Report 2018*. AI Now Institute at New York University.

Williams, Ronald J (1992). "Simple Statistical Gradient-Following Algorithms for Connectionist Reinforcement Learning". In: *Machine Learning* 8.3, pp. 229–256.

Wolf, Thomas et al. (2020). "Transformers: State-of-the-Art Natural Language Processing". In: *arXiv preprint arXiv:1910.03771*.

Yannakakis, Georgios N. and Julian Togelius (2018). *Artificial Intelligence and Games*. Springer.

Yosinski, Jason et al. (2014). "How Transferable are Features in Deep Neural Networks?" In: *Advances in Neural Information Processing Systems*. Vol. 27.

Yudkowsky, Eliezer (2008). "Artificial Intelligence as a Positive and Negative Factor in Global Risk". In: *Global Catastrophic Risks* 1, pp. 303–345.

Zafar, Muhammad Bilal et al. (2017). "Fairness Beyond Disparate Treatment & Disparate Impact: Learning Classification without Disparate Mistreatment". In: *Proceedings of the 26th International Conference on World Wide Web*, pp. 1171–1180.

Zhang, Chao et al. (2021). "Adversarial Privacy-preserving Voice Synthesis". In: *IEEE Transactions on Information Forensics and Security* 16, pp. 2347–2359.

Zhavoronkov, Alex et al. (2019). "Deep Learning Enables Rapid Identification of Potential Drug Targets for the COVID-19 Pandemic". In: *Nature Biotechnology*.

Zhu, Jun-Yan et al. (2017). "Unpaired Image-to-Image Translation using Cycle-Consistent Adversarial Networks". In: *Proceedings of the IEEE International Conference on Computer Vision*, pp. 2223–2232.

www.ingramcontent.com/pod-product-compliance
Lightning Source LLC
Chambersburg PA
CBHW042038230526
45474CB00005B/2